LOCAL LIVES IN A GLOBAL PANDEMIC:

Stories from North Central Florida

EDITED BY PAT CAREN, CHARLES R. COBB, RONNIE LOVLER, AND MALLORY M. O'CONNOR

Archway Publishing books may be ordered through booksellers or by contacting:

Archway Publishing
1663 Liberty Drive
Bloomington, IN 47403
www.archwaypublishing.com
844-669-3957

ISBN: 978-1-6657-1291-0 (sc)
ISBN: 978-1-6657-1292-7 (e)

Library of Congress Control Number: 2021919939

Print information available on the last page.

Archway Publishing rev. date: 10/12/2021

CONTENTS

ACKNOWLEDGMENTS

Our editorial team was fortunate to receive moral, logistical, and financial support from a number of directions. The members of our respective organizations, the Writers Alliance of Gainesville (WAG) and the Matheson History Museum, were enthusiastic advocates of this project from its inception. In addition, both WAG and the Matheson provided funding for this project. Other generous contributors included the City of Gainesville's Department of Parks, Recreation and Cultural Affairs; Russ Etling, Cultural Affairs Manager; and Satchel's Pizza through their Satch Grant program. This book could not have been completed without the assistance of this network of patrons, and we are grateful that they shared our vision of the importance of this work.

This project was inspired in part by the Matheson History Museum's "COVID Archives." This online portal (linked to the Matheson Museum website) was initiated in the early days of the pandemic, in spring 2020, by the Matheson curator, Kaitlyn Hof-Mahoney. Kaitlyn sent a call out for observations, reports, experiences, and images related to the COVID crisis, and she then collected and posted the responses in the COVID Archives. Many of those contributions are contained in this book. We owe Kaitlyn a debt of gratitude for her innovative work on the Archive and for the assistance she has provided to make that work available in this compilation.

Finally, we thank the many contributors represented in the pages that follow. They have given voice and image to one of the more devastating global events to have occurred in our lifetimes. Their experiences and insights reflect the strong sense of community that characterizes the Gainesville area and which we trust will lead us out of this crisis.

PREFACE: GENERATIONAL SHIFT

» BY LAUREN POE
MAYOR OF GAINESVILLE, FLORIDA

Generational shift, global shock, societal reset…These are all abstract terms people like me use to teach young people about life-changing historical events that impact us all. Most of us never predicted that pandemic would be on that list during our lifetimes. In hindsight, perhaps we should have.

Not one us was prepared for the tectonic shift to our daily lives that the COVID-19 pandemic would bring. We were suddenly and without grace forced into a new lifestyle uncontemplated and certainly unrehearsed.

Activities and responsibilities we took for granted suddenly disappeared or were radically altered. Work/life balance took on a whole new meaning and access to food or "delicacies" became a mix of strategy and blood sport. And unlike the occasional hurricane or winter storm, we had no idea when, or if, the end would come.

Through all of this anxiety, uncertainty, and dread arose a new Gainesville. Neighbors were peering over their fences for the first time and introducing themselves. Streets were clogged with neighbors strolling, ambling, and even sauntering. Children's melodies of outdoor adventure wafted through the air. People cooked a loaf of bread for the first time and prepared meals for their more vulnerable friends. And we all learned that masks are sexy!

Gainesville decided we were going to help each other out and we would have one another's backs. Never been a teacher? Here are some great resources! Tired of cooking? Here is how you can help support our local eating establishments and the thousands of people they employ. Need some culture? Here are some local online options, or you can visit one of our safe, socially-distanced outdoor offerings. We learned how to maintain, even grow, our sense of community while protecting one another's health.

In the short shadow of 2020, many of us still wonder what the "new-normal" will look like. What I do know is that Gainesville will emerge stronger, more unified, more innovative, creative, and more hopeful than we ever imagined. That is who we are, and no pandemic can take that away.

FOREWORD

» BY DIXIE NIELSON
EXECUTIVE DIRECTOR, MATHESON HISTORY MUSEUM

Most people view historians as those who study ancient cultures, or those who pour through dusty books looking to support a new theory on an old subject. Rarely do we think of historians as news reporters, and even less often as reporters of events that are happening here and now. But indeed, we are.

Although not much can be considered "golden" about the COVID-19 pandemic, it has presented us with an opportunity to tell a story of worldwide proportions, seen through the eyes of those in our own Alachua County community as it happens, day by day.

In early February 2020, before most of us were concerned about the onslaught of COVID-19, I was preparing to give a lecture on the impact of the 1918 Spanish Influenza on north Florida. In looking back at my notes now, the early reports I had read seem eerily familiar.

The Jacksonville newspapers reported that in mid-September 1918, 1000 cases of a mild flu was reported at a Michigan Naval Station, but Jacksonville's Camp Johnston proudly reported that there were only thirteen cases of flu and no deaths. Officials stated that there was no cause for concern; they expected the flu to be over within the month. The next day there were 181 new flu cases. Shortly thereafter, Duval County Schools were closed, indoor meetings were banned, dancehalls and pool rooms were closed. Even the Barnum and Bailey Circus was cancelled. A photograph from the State Archives shows nearly fifty school children in Starke, gathered for their class photograph, all wearing masks.

Nonetheless, newspapers reported on the approaching end of World War I and the sales of war bonds far more heavily than they did on the rising death toll due to what we now know was the Spanish Influenza. These were interesting facts, and informed my audience well enough, but that wasn't what I was looking for.

As a social historian, I wanted to hear the human side of the story. How did the general public react to this news? Was there a mass exodus from the cities to less populated areas? How did businesses survive? What precautions were put in place? Were they obeyed? Of course, today, a year later—it seems like a lifetime—I would have asked if fights broke out because people refused to wear their masks; were parties banned? Did they use the term super-spreader? But there were very few reports of affected individuals and their families.

In less than a month after my research, as we all hoped for the best, we saw more and more evidence that we were in serious trouble from this new COVID-19, and we were scared. Then our world closed. Every day new catchphrases popped up to calm us and help us deal with the isolation that this disease was imposing on us.

So, Gainesville set about to cope. Yard signs popped up saying those same phrases we grew so familiar with: You're not alone, We're in this together, Don't Panic, Wear Your Mask. The board and the staff of the Matheson History Museum came together to ask ourselves what we could do beyond repeating the same words which didn't give us much comfort.

We consider our institution THE community museum of Gainesville and beyond. As our tagline says, "We're *Your* Museum," and we really take that to heart. The people of Gainesville/Alachua County are our people. We have celebrated, grieved, honored, and put on display the important events of more than twenty-five years within our walls. Rather than just observe and record this history, we all felt we needed to *do* something. Almost simultaneously several of us had the same idea.

Saying "you are not alone" was not enough. We wanted to *show* how alike we all were in this worldwide catastrophe. We were all missing important events. We were all missing our loved ones. It seemed it would be more comforting to see the evidence that we were not going through this as individuals but as the community that we are.

We had the idea that someday in the future we would (safely) collect objects for a COVID-19 exhibit, but right now, this very minute, we could collect digital images to show each other what we were doing to navigate this new world. We advertised our idea and invited you all to send us your photos, your drawings, your poems, and songs. Thus, the COVID-19 Archive was born. Over two hundred of these personal stories came to us and have been preserved online on the Matheson Museum web page.

It was a wonderful effort that grew even more wonderful with the partnership between the Matheson History Museum and the Writer's Alliance of Gainesville (WAG) who together recorded these events in book form. Spearheaded by board member Ronnie Lovler and Curator Kaitlyn Hof-Mahoney on the Matheson team, and Mallory O'Connor and Pat Caren representing the WAG team, the City of Gainesville, and a Satch Grant from Satchel's Pizza, along with a whole lot of interns, volunteers, students, and of course all of you, we recorded history as it happened. May this publication keep some future historian from wondering what the people who lived through this pandemic thought and felt. We hope this publication will bring comfort to those who need it and serve as a long-term reminder that, indeed, we are not alone, and we have the book to prove it.

FOREWORD

» **BY PAT CAREN**
**PRESIDENT OF WRITERS ALLIANCE OF
GAINESVILLE (2019-2020)**

Other than a handful of epidemiologists, few had an inkling of what 2020 had in store for us. Diseases such as smallpox, the bubonic plague, and cholera were things of the past. Modern medicine had contained, if not conquered, such pestilences. Even the Spanish flu pandemic of 1918 was but a small chapter in the history books. Such things couldn't happen in the 21st century, could they?

Most of us were blindsided. Early in the year, when reports of a new coronavirus began to circulate and scientists warned us this could become a global pandemic, we thought, how bad could it really be? Recent decades had brought us scares: Ebola, SARS, dengue fever, Zika. These had caused deaths, certainly, but for relatively few people. Public health practices and medical care kept most of us safe. We expected the same with this new disease.

We weren't far into 2020 before our perceptions began to change. In late February, the Centers for Disease Control warned that everyday life could be disrupted. By early March, handshakes were out, elbow bumps were in. I attended a function where, instead of serving ourselves from the buffet, servers standing behind a Plexiglas barrier asked what we wanted and filled our plates for us. Travel was restricted. Rumors of quarantine began to circulate. Elderly people began to isolate themselves.

Mid-March, the world changed. Schools were closed. People were told to stay home and, if possible, work from home. Sports events were cancelled. I doubt science fiction writers could have foreseen what was in store for us. Even our language has changed. Social distancing has become a verb. "Stay safe" has replaced "Have a good day."

"May you live in interesting times." This is widely attributed to be a Chinese curse, although there is no evidence it originated in China. Whatever its origin, we do find ourselves in interesting times!

The Matheson History Museum in Gainesville decided to record history in the making and create an archive of the thoughts and experiences of ordinary people during this pandemic. A handful of community members contributed artwork, photography, and narrative accounts. The suggestion that these be complied in a book was made. Ronnie Lovler and Mallory O'Connor, who have connections with both the Matheson and the Writers Alliance of Gainesville, thought that local writers would be a good resource. As WAG president, I threw my lot in. Thus, a partnership was formed. University of Florida Professor Charlie Cobb, who is on the Matheson Board, joined our editorial team.

We sought contributions from a diverse spectrum of the community, writers and non-writers alike. The poetry in the book is terse with emotion. Victims describe their suffering. Medical people show us a window into their struggles. Young people decry being denied rites of passage such as prom and graduation, and they express fear for the safety of their loved ones. Teachers, parents, and grandparents give us their perspective, as well as public figures and even one prison inmate. Other than some necessary editing, these stories are presented in the storyteller's own words.

This collection has its shortcomings. The essays and poetry in the book do not represent a cross section of the community. Due to the voluntary nature of the submissions, some voices were left out despite efforts to recruit them. Working people have been thrown into poverty, and we can only imagine the plight of the homeless. On the positive side, some of the contributors have provided glimpses into the experiences of these silent voices.

Local Lives in a Global Pandemic: Stories from North Central Florida covers 2020 only, even though the pandemic has not yet passed its peak, but it is beyond the scope of the book to be a compete history of the COVID-19 experience. It is a snapshot, designed to give current readers an insight into the thoughts and feelings of their neighbors, and for future generations, a window into the real-time experiences of those who have lived through it.

EDITOR BIOGRAPHIES

Pat Caren is a retired teacher and social worker who studied Literature at Eckerd College and did graduate work at the University of Florida. She has been a member of the Writers Alliance of Gainesville since 2013 and has served on the board since 2017, including a term as President from 2019 to 2020. She is a member of Florida Writers Association and a judge for the Royal Palm Literary Award. In addition to her literary interests, she is a Master Gardener, a founding member of Alligator Creek Garden Club in Starke, and a member of Florida Wildflower Foundation. She loves to travel and writes under the name Marie Q Rogers.

Charles Cobb is a short-timer in Alachua County, having arrived with his wife and two cats on January 1, 2015. Having grown up as an Air Force "brat," this the latest—and hopefully last—of many migrations in his life. He has found serving on the Board of the Matheson Museum to be a wonderful opportunity for a crash course in the fascinating history of the region. Currently, he is a curator and archaeologist at the Florida Museum of Natural History. His hobbies include reading, overindulging in watching football, and enjoying the fruits of his wife's labors at beekeeping.

Ronnie Lovler is an award-winning journalist, a contributing writer for the *Gainesville Sun* and *Gainesville Magazine,* and a freelance writer and editor. She is also an adjunct professor at the University of Florida and Santa Fe College. She is on the boards of several local organizations, including the Matheson History Museum, the Writers Alliance of Gainesville, and the Civic Media Center. She is a former correspondent for CNN in Latin America and a contributing author in the anthology *Alone Together: Tales of Sisterhood and Solitude in Latin America.* She was also a Knight International Journalism Fellow in Colombia. She began her career in journalism at the *San Juan Star* in San Juan, Puerto Rico.

Award-winning author, Mallory M. O'Connor, holds degrees in art, art history, and American history from Ohio University. She taught art history at the University of Florida and Santa Fe College for over twenty years. Following her retirement in 2005, she wrote the *American River Trilogy* (Tributaries, Currents, and Confluence) and started a series of paranormal/occult thrillers, *Epiphany's Gift* (2019) and *Key to Eternity* (2020). Mallory lives with her artist husband, John A. O'Connor in Gainesville, Florida.

CHAPTER 1

THE VIRUS ARRIVES: LIFE DISRUPTED

Gainesville, FL
Morning
APRIL 11, 2020
Reported: 514,415
Deaths: 19,882

APRIL 11, 2020

"I began documenting the sky every morning since April 6, 2020. To make the pieces reflect the morning moment I would give myself approximately one hour. It didn't matter if the piece needed more time or just looked funky, I would stop. The pieces are how I felt at the time and what I saw."

– Gwendolyn Chrzanowski

ALACHUA COUNTY STAY AT-HOME-ORDER

» BY RONNIE LOVLER

Today was Day 1 of the Official Stay-at-Home order in Alachua County. The biggest change I noticed was at the supermarket. A police officer stood watch to make sure only forty-five people went into the store at a time. On the sidewalk, "X" marked the spot for the line outside to indicate where people should stand to stay six feet apart. Of course, my outing provoked scoldings from my two sons who were aghast that I had ventured out. I will concede, they are probably right.

But other than that, it hasn't been that different from the previous week when I observed an unofficial stay-at-home policy. I went out for a walk in the morning to my favorite walking trail. Fellow walkers posted words of encouragement on the trail, like a signpost that urged walkers (and runners) to stay focused and sparkly.

On occasion I saw a deer or many deer alongside the trail. They hadn't gotten the word about social distancing or staying in small groups. They were a nice surprise for the morning.

At home, online. Almost always. My classes at the University of Florida and at Santa Fe College went from in-person to online. Now I am learning new tools about online teaching that I never expected to learn, or even really wanted to learn. Our brave new world is Zooming.

That's Zoom, the new video-conferencing tool that is taking over academia and the non-profit world. I have been on Zoom conferences about a dozen times in the past few days. I have given two classes on Zoom. But I am zoomed out now for the day and about to visit my local bar—the one in my living room, that is. Staying at home is exhausting. Time for a break.

*The Alachua County stay-at-home order went into effect at midnight, March 24, 2020.

Ronnie Lovler is one of the editors of this book and an award-winning journalist and freelance writer and editor. A former correspondent for CNN in Latin America, she is also an adjunct professor at the University of Florida and Santa Fe College. She is active in the community, serving on the boards of several organizations, including the Matheson History Museum and the Writers Alliance of Gainesville.

LIVING UNDERCOVER: COVID-19 MASKS

» BY BONNIE OGLE

For the next hundred years, say "2020" and everyone's first thought will be: COVID-19. The word evokes the collective experience of those lucky enough to have survived it—worry, depression, loneliness. Overwhelmed, we watch the news, full of dismal tidings edging around the pandemic: Black Lives Matter marches hijacked by rioters and looters, horrific wildfires and destructive hurricanes and flooding, politics that reached new lows.

In its midst, we want to turn it off, get up and go . . . somewhere, anywhere . . . to escape. But first, where did I put that mask? It's ironic that the top-rated television show of 2020 is *The Masked Singer*. How appropriate.

Our heroes used to be veterans and Olympians. They still are, but front-line workers are our new champions: clerks, custodians, deliverymen, waitresses, bus drivers. Those who rarely got a nod of thanks now don masks and put themselves in jeopardy to help others. They may not want to or like wearing a mask for eight hours, but they do it. It may just be self-protection, or job preservation, but it is a responsibility to protect ourselves and others.

The CDC and World Health Organization say cloth facemasks are a critical tool in the fight against COVID spread. Of course, you have to wear it correctly. Over your mouth *and* your nose.

In the beginning, it was hard to find masks. Like many of my acquaintances, I made them for friends and family. A quilter, I had amassed a variety of fabrics. I ran out of elastic and so did every store in the county. We found a multitude of patterns online. Now you can spend up to fifteen dollars for a custom mask promoting your favorite team, hobby, or political candidate. Cloth masks are easily washable and rarely end up as litter, which paper masks do.

Masks arouse considerable dissension. Many refuse to wear one. Multiple myths have risen. Some think added resistance to air flow limits oxygen intake. Not true, unless you have an underlying respiratory condition. In addition to discomfort, some believe cloth masks are not effective at all. Experts say they are highly so for the general public, those not working in a medical environment.

I don't need to take up scarce surgical masks or N95 Respirators. These are critical for health care workers. Living in a community with major hospitals, I see friends leaving their families to serve an at-risk population, and yes, ministering to COVID patients. My late husband was a first responder. Their job entails far more exposure to danger from medical runs than fighting fires.

I have otherwise intelligent friends who think if they're asymptomatic, they needn't wear a mask. Other friends think, "Oh, I'm not at risk." Studies show asymptomatic carriers can increase the disease's spread if they aren't taking proper precautions, including wearing a mask and social distancing.

Differing opinions on that issue affect relationships. My brother declined an invitation to the neighbor's pool party. Within days the entire sociable family was diagnosed with COVID-19. I repeatedly declined invitations to weekends at a beach house with a friend's extended family. I almost wished they'd get it, then I prayed for forgiveness.

I now understand "COVID shaming," a popular social put down that's cropped up on social media, like the guy screaming in capital letters on Facebook that he wasn't going to wear a face mask, then within months, posting he'd tested positive for COVID. Weeks later, family members announced his death. Hundreds of ha-ha laughing face emojis responded, along with critical "serves him right" comments.

I miss live time with my friends and loved ones and a sense of normalcy. I do see the unmasked faces of fellow members of the Writers Alliance on our weekly Zoom meetings, but it lacks the warmth of live meetings. Work with children at the Florida Museum has stopped. Missing live worship, I attended a nearby church requiring pre-registration and masks. Once I entered the sanctuary, I saw no masks. Back to online worship until my own church reopens! Ballroom dance classes seem risky, even with temperature checks. Dancing in other people's arms, even with a mask, seems like tempting fate.

So what do we do? Being outside is generally considered safer than being inside. Getting my hands in dirt is therapeutic. My garden never looked so beautiful. Biking and walking are great outdoor exercise and I've met some nice people. Such outdoor activities, alone or with people you live with, don't require a mask. There are many outdoor dining venues I enjoy with friends. It's kind of hard to wear a mask and eat, so take-out and dining on the porch are safe alternatives.

Finding help from our leaders is futile. Our own state governor, Ron DeSantis, was the first to open beaches. In September, he reopened bars and restaurants at full capacity. This, despite Florida's continuing rise in cases and deaths. The president mostly refused to wear a mask and even accused one reporter of being "politically correct" for declining to take off his mask to ask a question. He continually belittled his opponent Joe Biden for wearing a mask, and leading up to the November election, he continued to hold densely packed rallies where most supporters were not wearing masks. Until he contracted the virus himself, bringing COVID shaming—and political vitriol—to a new low.

A hodgepodge of city and county ordinances address masks. Causing some confusion, the governor banned the collection of fines and penalties moving into Phase 3 of reopening in September. He also clamped down on state universities which threatened expulsion to students hosting large gatherings.

For a while, businesses required masks for entry. There were Xs on the floor at my local Publix and employees counting entrants, while they cleaned grocery carts. The Xs are gone now, and about half of the shoppers are not wearing masks. Maybe because there was an incident where a gun-wearing shopper refused to wear a mask. He became so rowdy, police were called.

The coronavirus is projected to kill more than 400,000 Americans by the end of this year.

Most of us, by now, know someone who has contracted it, or worse, did not survive.

I'm not a leader or a doctor. So what can I do? I CAN WEAR A MASK AND SOCIAL DISTANCE. It requires some sacrifice and discomfort. I can pray for the researchers, the victims and their families, and for discernment for mayors, governors, and the president. And for those on the front line, I can show my appreciation by wearing my mask.

Bonnie T. Ogle is a retired public school teacher, now a teacher and docent at the Florida Museum of Natural History. She is a volunteer interpreter at the McGuire Center for Lepidoptera. Memberships include Word Weavers International, The Writers Alliance of Gainesville, and lifetime memberships in Phi Kappa Phi Educational Honor Society, and Girl Scouts USA. Her published works include *Pledge Allegiance with the Pledge Rap*, *The Sounds and Smells of Christmas*, and *Arthur the Arthropod*.

(PHOTO BY ANN SMITH)

"Public parks, including this one in Jonesville, have closed down during the pandemic. Officials have closed off the playground equipment and facilities because they do not allow for adequate social distancing or sanitization in between use."

– Ann Smith, retired nurse

MUSIC INTERRUPTED

» **BY FRANK CURTIS**

I've been a member of the Gainesville Community Band since 1991. Before that time, I had never stepped into a band room or played an instrument. I was a thirty-year-old whose life had made several serious unforeseen changes. I chose to work at a Gainesville music store called Band Central Station. Selling and repairing instruments daily helped me to learn some basics.

One afternoon, a nice lady came into the store and wanted to buy a saxophone for her husband. "I play sax, too," I told her with great enthusiasm. "My dream saxophone would be this one right here. It's easy to play, and the best sound I've ever heard." She agreed to buy the saxophone under the condition I join the Gainesville Community Band. My heart took a grand pause and missed a few beats. I countered, "Lady, I've never even been in a band room."

She said, "That's okay, my husband hasn't played since high school. So, are you going to join the band?"

The rest is history. All three of us are still in the band, but unfortunately, we have not been able to play together since March of 2020.

The Gainesville Community Band was founded in 1974 with eleven members. In 1978, the Gainesville City Commission passed a resolution designating the Gainesville Community Band as the official community band of Gainesville. The Band is a member of the Association of Concert Bands. It is funded by a diverse group of patrons and sponsors and is an all-volunteer, non-profit organization. With a current a roster of about eighty members, the Band is made up of teachers, professors, scientists, business professionals, students, physicians, contractors, realtors, and retirees. Several professional musicians, who perform with other area groups, volunteer their talents with the Gainesville Community Band. The Director is University of Florida Professor Gary Langford, who took over from Dr. Gerald Poe in 2014. Dr. Poe conducted the band from 2004 to 2014, having assumed the baton from Santa Fe College's Richard Hord, the Band's conductor for over twenty-five years.

To even think that the COVID-19 virus hasn't affected myself and the nearly eighty other band members, not to mention our loyal audiences, is a far cry from our experience. As I write this, we would, in normal times, be gearing up for our annual Holiday Concert in December. As far as I know, this concert has never been cancelled. But we knew we had to suspend our musical efforts. We recognized the risks to our entire community and the Gainesville Community Band itself.

The Band usually performs at Fanfare and Fireworks, an event held at the Band Shell on the University of Florida campus on July 3rd, to celebrate the birth of our great nation. The hour-long concert at twilight ends with our national march, "Stars and Stripes Forever." This event has been a favorite of the community for over a quarter of a century, attracting an audience of more than 20,000 people each year. This year it was canceled, for good reasons, but sad for everyone.

The James B. King Veterans Day Concert was also canceled this year. King was a native of Charleston, South Carolina, and attended Curtis Institute of Music in Philadelphia. He enlisted in the Army where he performed on troop ships crossing the Atlantic during World War II. In 1946, Jim joined the Marine Band. He served as principal clarinet and assistant conductor at the White House until his retirement in 1968. Jim and his wife Joy were members of the Gainesville Community Band for twenty-six years. He died in October 2006, and the Band presents a Free Clarinet in his honor to a local middle school student. Teachers submit names of those students deserving this honor, in memory of this great musician who served his country so well. Band Central Station, Great Southern Music, and Hoggtowne Music have graciously donated the memorial clarinets at this event. Until now.

The Charles Dean Trumpet Memorial Concert was also canceled due to COVID-19. Charles Dean was born in Monticello, Florida. His only training was by his high school band director. In college, he majored in agriculture and played in dance bands, which enabled him to buy his first professional line trumpet. He joined the Fort Jackson Army Band after graduation. With a PhD in Plant Breeding and Genetics, Charlie was hired by the University of Florida in 1967. He became chairman of the Department of Agronomy in 1979, a position he held until his death in 1992. Charlie served as principal trumpet of the Gainesville Community Band for eighteen years. At this concert, which opens our season each year, we present a new trumpet to a deserving middle school trumpet player in Charlie's memory. These trumpets have also been provided by local music stores for decades.

Yes, we have been saddened that we have not been able to play our music and be together, to play our instruments for all of you in our wonderful community. We're also unhappy that we cannot show the musical way to the next generation, for now. We are, however, not defeated. We will patiently practice at home and even make some music together in the virtual world in 2020. We wish you all health, happiness, and looking forward to new possibilities for more music soon.

Frank Curtis is an award-winning artist, musician, book illustrator, and author who has created in our community since the 1970s. A graduate of Florida School of the Arts, Santa Fe College, University of Florida, and a USF Master's Candidate, his works reside in many private art collections and have been shown around the country. Currently Director of Artwalk Gainesville and President of the Arts Association of Alachua County, he has served the Gainesville Fine Arts Association in many capacities and is on the Gainesville Community Band Board. He plays saxophone, is a curator of art shows, and looks forward to doing more writing.

DELAYED BOOK LAUNCH

» **BY STEPHANIE A. SMITH**

I think this is a fabulous idea—document the pandemic, locally. So, my partner and I consider ourselves more than fortunate. We are both on the other side of 55, in fairly good health, and work at the University of Florida (UF); but I have chronic asthma, so I got worried very early on. Having lived in Berkeley through the HIV/AIDS insanity, I knew COVID-19 was going to be bad when Tony Fauci said it was going to be bad. He was one of the voices of truth back then, and now, again. So I self-quarantine the day before UF went online (I teach at UF). I was Zooming the week before the whole school went to Zoom.

Being a writer and fairly reclusive, my life hasn't changed drastically except for the fact that my book launch this year is not going to happen the way it should; I was supposed to go to New York City for the launch. And I love local restaurants and can't go out to see my friends at Dragonfly, Paramount Grille, Mildred's, Ichiban, Northwest Grille, etc. and local favorite shops and businesses like Nature Day Pet's Spa. But we've been using The Bite Squad to order from local businesses (particularly fond of Volcanic Sushi); we've been using Shipt and Instacart for grocery deliveries (thank you, thank you, thank you!) and online resources like Chewy for the dogs and cats and my standard monthly order from Grove (which has been delivering paper goods, thank goodness). But the best part has been local farms delivering produce and even meat to the door: thank you Swallowtail, Frog Song Organics, Rosie's Organic Farm, and The Old-Fashioned Farmstead for the fabulous produce, eggs, pork, and duck, and all the beautiful flowers, to keep us cheerful.

Though I miss my students, I miss being able to travel, particularly to the beach and to see my family in other states. I am not willing to go out until there are therapies and a vaccine, or until I know for a fact that the transmission has gone way, way down, or until I can get a test. To walk the dogs, I made myself a homemade mask, but I've ordered a more solid one for later this year. Since we had ourselves prepared for hurricane season, we have gloves, sanitizers, lots of canned goods, etc. stocked in already...so we are doing well, compared to many people, like my brother in NYC, listening to the wail of sirens every night.

Stephanie A. Smith took a PhD from UC Berkeley; she is currently an English Professor at the University of Florida, and is the author of the novels *Asteroidea* (Adelaide Books, 2020), *The Warpaint Trilogy* (2012-14), *Other Nature* (1995-7), *The-Boy-Who-Was-Thrown-Away* and *Snow-Eyes* (1985/87); criticism *Conceived By Liberty* (Cornell 1995) and *Household Words* (Minnesota, 2006); short stories in *New Letters*, *Asimov's* and *SF&F.*; creative non-fiction and numerous essays in journals such as *differences*, *American Literature*, and *Genre*; her next novel, *Strange Grace*, is forthcoming in 2021 (Adelaide Books).

HOMEMADE MASK (PHOTO BY STEPHANIE SMITH).

SPRING BIRD MIGRATION IN ALACHUA COUNTY DURING COVID-19

» BY DEBRA SEGAL

Springtime is when birds fly from their wintering haunts in Central and South America to their breeding grounds in Canada and the northern reaches of the United States. During this marathon spring journey, which generally occurs in April and early May, millions of birds wing their way northward, flying thousands of miles at night over land and across oceans, and sometimes through treacherous storms, to reach their summer breeding grounds.

Some of the colorful warblers, tanagers, grosbeaks, and thrushes—clad in their most eye-popping breeding plumage—descend into the woods of Gainesville to refuel on insects, seeds, and berries before completing their miraculous long-distance migration. For the Alachua Audubon Society and birding groups throughout the country, April and early May mark one of the most exciting and highly anticipated periods in which to immerse in nature and the exciting world of birds.

"Unaffected and completely oblivious to the 2020 Coronavirus, migrating birds paused in Alachua County during their marathon journey in unusually high numbers."

– Debra Segal

COVID-19 struck just as bird watchers in Alachua County and around the country were anxiously awaiting spring migration. In mid-March, when cancellations of gatherings of all sorts were announced and social distancing mandates were enacted, the Alachua Audubon Society followed suit and canceled all of its planned spring birding events, including those outings that specifically targeted a glimpse of the colorful and rare spring migrants.

How are bird watchers coping with the pandemic? Many folks spruced up their yards by adding more native plants, bird feeders, and water features and have occupied themselves with observing, admiring, and photographing their avian visitors. Others, armed with binoculars, ventured out alone or in pairs to natural areas in search of rare spring migrants.

To prevent unsafe gatherings, state and local land managers closed many parks and nature centers including favorite birding hotspots such as Paynes Prairie Preserve State Park, San Felasco Hammock State Park, and Bivens Arm Nature Center. Other parks that allow for visitors to spread out and avoid congregating, such as Sweetwater Wetlands Park, Hogtown Creek Greenway, and Prairie Creek Preserve, remained open during the pandemic and provided an escape to nature for Alachua County residents. Those and other accessible areas presented the backdrop to safely observe birds and nature during the economic and social shutdown.

Unaffected and completely oblivious to the 2020 Coronavirus, migrating birds paused in Alachua County during their marathon journey in unusually high numbers. Cape May, Blackpoll, and Bay-breasted Warblers; Scarlet Tanagers; Rose-breasted Grosbeaks; and various thrushes all showed up in greater abundance than anticipated.

We can only speculate on the better-than-expected spring migration that presented itself in Alachua County in April and early May of 2020. One likely explanation is that more and greater intensity spring storms blew additional migrants into central Florida, when normally they would fly north over the Gulf to their northern destinations.

And since the pandemic has prevented many people from going to work, some of the grounded bird watchers have spent part of their furlough searching for birds. More eyes scanning trees and lakes can certainly translate into an upsurge in the discovery of rare birds.

Bird watchers in Alachua County discovered a colorful silver lining during the frightening, lifestyle-altering pandemic that gripped the nation during the spring of 2020—the opportunity to admire some of the lovely northern birds and a glimpse into the fascinating life history of long-distance migrants.

Debbie Segal, 60, is a retired Environmental Scientist and current President of the Alachua Audubon Society.

CELEBRATING IN SPITE OF CORONAVIRUS

» **BY MARIE Q ROGERS**

My mother, who lives in Arkansas, turned ninety in September, 2020. We had plans for her birthday. I come from a large family and we are scattered around the globe, from Florida, across the South, to Oklahoma, Washington, and Djibouti in East Africa. Despite family reunions every two years, getting us ALL together at one time is no small feat.

But not impossible. Dad had turned eighty in November, 2006. Months of planning went into his birthday celebration. My sisters and I had a good time just getting there. Several of us met in Florida and drove to Arkansas together, doing a little sightseeing along the way. We stopped in Vicksburg one night and, before crossing the Mississippi River into Arkansas the next day, we toured the McRaven House (said to be the most haunted house in Mississippi).

On the morning of Dad's birthday, we all showed up on his doorstep. Not only surprised, Dad was brought to tears. We spent the whole day together, just Dad, Mom, and their children, visiting and feasting.

We were glad we didn't wait. The next time we came together was for his funeral, less than two years later.

In 2010, Mom knew we planned a similar celebration for her eightieth birthday. She let us know ahead of time that she didn't want a big fuss. By her request, we took her out to eat at the Queen Wilhelmina State Park Restaurant on Rich Mountain near Mena, Arkansas. Ten years later, as her ninetieth birthday approached, we started to make plans.

Then COVID. When everything shut down in March, the future became uncertain. We continued tentative plans, hoping that by summer the situation would improve. It didn't. Americans became pariahs in many parts of the world. My sister in Djibouti cancelled her travel plans. She was afraid if she tried to fly home, she might get stuck somewhere in quarantine. Worse, if she made it to the States, she might not be able to get back to Djibouti.

A major consideration was our mother's health. Florida was a COVID hot spot. Did we dare bring our germs to her from all over the country?

Every time I called her, Mom said to stay home. She told everyone else the same. Sadly, we agreed this was best. Maybe we could get together for her ninety-first.

Zoom to the rescue. All my meetings were now on Zoom. For months, I'd had no personal contact with anyone but masked store clerks and my immediate family. The same with the rest of the world. Why not a Zoom get-together?

I emailed all my siblings. Getting some of them to respond to an email, even a phone call, was an undertaking. Those who didn't respond had spouses who did. Everyone was on board. Next hurdle—Mom has no internet and the signal in the Blackfork Valley is weak in most places. After several phone calls to my somewhat tech-savvy brother-in-law, we found a solution. Because of its proximity to the phone company building, the Blackfork Volunteer Fire Department has a good internet signal. It helps to have relatives in the fire department.

What time? We had four different time zones to deal with. We decided on noon Eastern, which would be 11am Central Time, 9am Pacific, and 8pm in Djibouti. No one had to get up in the middle of the night. I set up a Zoom meeting, using the free plan.

On the morning of her birthday, my local siblings scooped Mom up and took her to the firehouse. I don't know what they told her, but she had to be suspicious of something. I don't think she had any idea she would be able to talk face to face with all her children on her birthday.

One by one, everyone tuned in. Our youngest brother was late, so we started telling stories about things he did when he was a little kid. His ears must have been buzzing. When he joined us, we changed the subject. There was no agenda. We sang "Happy Birthday," then just chatted. It was almost as good as being together in the same room.

Mom kept asking how much this was costing me. I assured her it was free. I also warned everyone that we had only forty-five minutes. Before the time was up, a message came on the screen that our time was being extended. I don't know why. Maybe it was a slow day for Zoom. My oldest brother and his wife were traveling, using their cell phone. They must have lost their signal, because they froze. The rest of us visited for over an hour and a half before Mom got tired and we decided it was enough for the day.

It was so nice to see everyone and just talk about ordinary things, catch up on news. Since then, every time I've called Mom, she tells me how much she enjoyed it.

The coronavirus has taken much from us, but it has kick-started creative thinking. We have found new ways to accomplish old things. I hope the virus is gone by next September so my family can get together in person for our mother's birthday. It will be nice to share a real cake, not just a virtual one. But whatever fate throws at us, we will find a way.

Marie Q Rogers is an award-winning author who lives and writes in the woods of North Florida. Her Young Adult novel, *Trials by Fire*, received a 2020 Royal Palm Literary Award. She is currently juggling three or four other novels in various stages of completion. Her work has appeared in *Bacopa Literary Review* and *Pilcrow & Dagger*, and she posts creative non-fiction on her weblog, marieqrogers.com.

INTERVIEW WITH DR. PAUL ORTIZ

» **PROFESSOR OF HISTORY AT THE UNIVERSITY OF FLORIDA (CONDUCTED BY RONNIE LOVLER, MATHESON HISTORY MUSEUM, NOVEMBER 27, 2020)**

Ronnie Lovler: In general, how did COVID impact you and the people you serve? Paul Ortiz: It had a profound impact. In the course I was teaching in the spring, we switched to remote learning pretty quickly. Right away, a number of my students contracted the coronavirus and it had a big impact on their learning.

A lot of teaching and instructional faculty, you know, have pre-existing health conditions, like pulmonary issues, and so forth.

The virus impacted everyone around me pretty quickly. You know, my father just turned eighty-two. Obviously, he couldn't travel anymore. He's a military veteran. He has a lung full of asbestos and Agent Orange. So we have to be so careful with his health.

RL: Can you provide some specific examples of how COVID made things more difficult for you?

PO: For my students, we had to pretty much throw out the syllabus, deadlines, and normal benchmarks, because I would get a doctor's note from a student and they would be in bed rest for a week. And the other really disturbing thing is that the virus has lingering health effects on their ability to really kind of focus. So extended papers, especially like senior theses, seminar papers, are key for them to try to get ready for grad school or law school or the job market.

I also became president of the Faculty Union on May first, and from that time, I'm getting eight to ten calls per day from sometimes very distraught colleagues, because the University of Florida has been trying to push people back onto campus. We have a very unsafe campus. We have a lot of students who respect protocols and who wear masks and do social distancing. But we also have a lot of students who party and don't wear masks and are very proud about not wearing masks. So we have to be so careful on campus right now, it's like walking on eggshells.

RL: I didn't realize that you had just come on as President of the [Union] Faculty in May. So you actually began with the pandemic?

PO: Not the best timing. There's a number of faculty who are in their the mid to late sixties, who planned to teach another five or ten years, and now they've just decided they're going to hang it up and retire. It's really going to hurt this campus.

We did the right thing in the spring when the virus first hit. We shut the campus down and we essentially told the students, go home, and take the courses remotely. But towards the end of the summer, we got the word. Oh, well, now we want you to go back to class. And I think what happened was our administration bet on the wrong horse in terms of the election. I think they thought Donald Trump was going to have a pretty resounding victory and I think that's why they thought pushing us back into the classroom would have political benefits.

So what we're trying to deal with is defending our members unit by unit. What I mean by this is that we have members who have recently had children or are pregnant. They have diabetes or they have a pulmonary situation, and they cannot go back into a classroom. And so we're literally fighting department by department, unit by unit, to try to keep them teaching and working and counseling remotely. What I've been trying to do is, as Union president, is to try to let everyone know, especially off campus, that we're working as hard as ever. It's just that we're working differently.

RL: How many members of the faculty are in their sixties, or in the age bracket that is considered high risk?

PO: I think teaching is so experiential. I don't think anyone is born a good teacher. I think you learn how to become a teacher over time. That's why I think losing older faculty is especially devastating because it is the older faculty who mentor us how to teach and socialize us and show us the ropes. You know, they… they give us a sense of what the culture is. When you lose that experience you've lost a lot. And that makes it much harder for us to sustain our intellectual communities here.

RL: How has COVID affected you personally?

PO: It terrifies me. My wife has a number of health conditions. My father has very fragile health. There's a lot of elders in my family. So it's really, it's caused a lot of stress. We did a family Zoom for Thanksgiving. It's more important to keep each other healthy than it is to travel right now.

I have mixed feelings about Zoom. But on the other hand, it really has helped us.

RL: Did you gain anything from your COVID experiences that will help you and your organization going forward?

PO: In the oral history program, we rely on human interaction, talking to people. Doing fieldwork—that's kind of the bread and butter. So we've had to maintain close contact through the phone, through Zoom, through letters.

I think it's brought us, you know, closer in some ways, we don't take for granted the friendships we've built over the years. I think, if anything that's a positive. I think the other positive impact I can mention is humility. I hope that more people in this culture gain a sense of humility, which was something we were grievously lacking beforehand. What I mean by this is that I have a lot of former students who live in other countries; you know, say, Taiwan, Mexico, and New Zealand. Almost any country on earth has done better than the U.S. in terms of dealing with the coronavirus, and listening and hoping that we will learn.

I think more Americans are saying, well, you know, maybe this isn't a natural disaster. Maybe it could have been different, you know, maybe we could do things differently in the society. Maybe we should. I hear more people, for example, saying, maybe we should have a single payer healthcare system. You know, it just doesn't make sense to continue to ration healthcare, the way we do it. James Baldwin years ago said that Americans just refuse to look in the mirror, and one thing this viruses is doing is to cause us to look in the mirror.

RL: How did COVID impact faculty organizing?

PO: COVID really impacted faculty organizing because the first thing that faculty realized, especially when you have tried to push people back into the classroom, was that without collective bargaining, without representation in this campus, you're lost.

What I mean—I would talk to some faculty and they would say, "Well, Paul, you know, I respect what the Union is doing, but I don't really need it myself."

All of a sudden, a lot of people started joining because, they said, "You know, I really need representation. You know, my chair is telling me I have to be back in my office, you know, starting next Monday. Can you guys help me?" And we'd say, well, you know, if you're a member of the Union, we could help you a lot easier.

So, yes, it really has. It has impacted faculty organizing. I think it's made us, maybe easier for us to make the pitch that faculty are workers like anyone else. And yes, we have a certain privileged position, but when push comes to shove, the jobs we do are very political.

RL: What made you get involved with the issues of reopening or not reopening the campus?

PO: In the spring it became apparent that the life and well-being of our faculty and staff became really dependent upon us becoming more active. And so, right away, the Faculty Union got in the mix, with trying to work with… with as many units as we could to help develop safety protocols.

I feel like we did a fairly good job in the sense that we were able to work with a lot of units and emphasize to people that the faculty here are working really hard to change the mode of their teaching. And so we can make the case that we weren't going to harm instructional quality by teaching remotely. And so what we were able to do is, working with administration, is really reduce the percentage of in-person courses.

And so, in spite of all of the problems, and this kind of gets back right into the role of the Faculty Union, we made the case that we can do our jobs. We're working just as hard as ever, but we don't want to risk our lives in order to do our jobs. It seems kind of self-defeating.

RL: What has been the response of the UF Administration?

PO: Chaos, confused. We started asking, please share with us the mandate that's telling us from the state that we need to get back into face-to-face teaching. And they would say, well, it's there somewhere. We'll get it to you eventually, and they never got it to us. And then finally, right in the middle of a news conference, I got a note from the administration, from the board of governors, which has authority over the entire university system. The message was that they were strongly encouraging colleges and universities, where possible, to move towards face-to-face teaching. Not a mandate, not anywhere near a mandate, and so a lot of confusion.

But I don't want to just put it just on the UF administration. I think there's been a general failure in the society among leaders of institutions, corporations, healthcare companies, and universities. I'm not saying it's everywhere, but it is just in so many places.

This is the one time we needed people to be leaders. This is the one time we need people to care about each other's health, and we came up short. I just hope we can use it as a learning experience.

RL: Did the Faculty Union stance make the UF administration more cautious and careful in their approach?

PO: I do think we've had an impact. I hope that people in the community know that we want to have their backs, because the community is what makes this university work for generations. And I just hope that now we can kind of wake up and realize, hey, the university is about the entire community. And I'm hoping that's the one positive thing that we're going to get from this, this coronavirus crisis.

CHAPTER 2

VICTIMS AND FRONT-LINE WORKERS

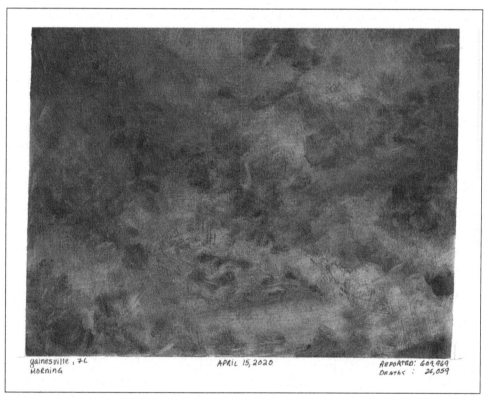

gainesville, FL
Morning   APRIL 15, 2020   REPORTED: 609,969
                                                             DEATHS : 26,059

APRIL 15, 2020 (GWENDOLYN CHRZANOWSKI)

PERSONAL NARRATIVE OF A COVID-19 SURVIVOR

» BY RANDY THORP

I was hospitalized for twenty-two days. I have emphysema and am lucky to have survived! I owe this in part to my partner, Annette Merritt,

I have an almost perpetual cough from COPD, but I never run a fever. Since fever is a hallmark of the disease, I began taking my temp several times a day. Sure enough, on the afternoon of Monday, March 16th, it was 100.5. Immediately, I went to a hotel to get away from Annette and her grandsons, whom she watches while their parents work. I called my regular doc, who said if symptoms worsened, go to the Emergency Room, not his office.

On Tuesday, I had more trouble breathing and my fever climbed to 102, so off to the ER. They gave me fluids and stuck swabs up my nose far enough to touch my brain. They sent one test to Jax [Jacksonville, FL] for analysis and did others in-house for flu. Negative for flu. After they got my fever down, they sent me home. The next day was worse, fever 103+, shaking, extreme difficulty breathing, so back to the ER.

They couldn't find me a room until after midnight, Thursday the 19th, on the sixth floor with other possible COVID folks. After a couple of days, the results of my tests came back positive and I was moved to the ICU and put on oxygen and Tylenol for fever (other NSAIDS can worsen COVID).

I had terrifying episodes during which I felt like I was drowning. The nurses and Annette (on the phone) got me through them. I asked my favorite nurses, Mae and Ana, if they were waiting for a real crisis to intubate me, and they said yes. Was there much doubt the crisis was, indeed, coming? No. So I asked to be intubated then, to be better prepared for the crisis when it came.

They told me I'd be sedated most of the time and awakened a couple times a day to be sure I was still there. Sounded good to me, but every time they tried to sedate me, my blood pressure tanked. So I was pretty much awake for the entire eight days the tubes were in.

It was not pleasant.

There were times when Annette got wonderful, up-beat reports from my nurses, but awful reports from me, because of the horrible fifteen to thirty minute periods when I totally panicked—it felt like I couldn't breathe and was dying. I would try frantically to take a big breath but couldn't. The nurses knew that as long as I was on the ventilator I couldn't suffocate. They would up my sedation (Seroquel, fentanyl, oxycodone, Xanax) until I got past the crisis. I will have nightmares about these periods, remembering them even when awake.

During these episodes, I couldn't take the deep breath I wanted because of the ventilator settings. My lungs were kept 85% inflated to keep them from collapsing. Only 15% was left for Inhalation and exhalation. No deep breath was possible. I couldn't feel it when my lungs were being inflated, but if I paid attention, I could feel the pressure let off for exhalation. So I'd exhale as hard as I could, which gave me room for a reasonable inhalation when the cycle restarted. At least I had some control!

Seroquel is an interesting drug, an anti-psychotic, used for manic depression and schizophrenia! But it brings acceptance of the current situation, whatever that might be. They called it a "compliance" drug. Anyway, it was quite effective.

I was also on the anti-malarial drug hydroxychloroquine, combined with Zithromycin. The problem is, the anti-malarial caused bad headaches, so Tylenol to the rescue again. How my days went was tied to getting meds every four hours on the dot! Even the "drowning" episodes were much less frequent when I got the drugs on schedule. But the nurses were frequently busy with other patients in crisis, so I was not top priority.

After eight days of intubation, I passed some milestone that I don't really understand, and they took out the tube. It was creepy. The tube goes past your vocal cords and then inflates to hold it in place. They just sort of deflated the ring and yanked it out. All sorts of noxious mucous and blood came with it but was quickly suctioned away. It felt so good! I was moved out of ICU. All that remained was to wait for two negative swabs taken more than twenty-four hours apart. After twenty-two days in the hospital, eleven in ICU, and eight intubated, Annette took me home!

A lot has been published about fear of dying alone, but I never felt alone. Annette communicated with me every single day, by phone when I could talk and by text when I couldn't. Pix of Mikey and Jacob cheered me up. Annette told me about support from friends and from people we barely knew. Karen Axelrod organized mini-concerts for me! The boys made pictures for me and neighborhood children left flowers on the porch. Annette was with me every step, every day. I would not have made it otherwise. And I was blessed with the absolute best of nurses.

When Annette picked me up at the hospital on April eighth, we decided I should be isolated for two weeks after my final negative swab, on April fifth. So I stayed in the master bedroom and bathroom and on the front porch. It was a lot of extra work for Annette. She had to fix my lunch and make sure I had everything I needed before she left each morning to care for the boys at their house. When she came home in the evening she had to fix dinner along with all the chores. But we got to eat together and visit on the porch. We could greet neighbors passing on the sidewalk, I spent most of my days on the front porch, reading and visiting online. I would have gone nuts without being able to enjoy the outdoors!

At first I was so weak that walking into the house from the car totally exhausted me. Taking a shower, even with the chair to sit on, was an ordeal, as was just getting to the bathroom. I weighed 160 pounds going in, 144 when I came out. My appetite came back, and I rejoiced to drink a cold beer!

My main worry was my cough. Starting the minute they removed the ventilator tubes, I had a persistent, very productive cough. It continued in the hospital and after I returned home. I didn't go fifteen minutes without coughing.

In a tele-session, my pulmonologist said he wasn't worried because I had had so many antibiotics while hospitalized, the mucus was clear, and there was no fever. He said that as my lungs healed from COVID-associated damage and pneumonia, a lot of mucus would be generated and would need to come out. He advised me to check my temp daily, but in the absence of a fever, not to worry. It would eventually go away. Finally, it did! Pretty much overnight. My wind is nearly as good as ever, considering my COPD.

I started physical therapy while isolated in the bedroom. I really like my PT guy! He started me on in-bed exercises, then moved me to more vigorous exercise on the porch. I'm getting close to where I was before getting sick. I now walk a couple of miles a day, along with my exercise routine. I can make trips to the grocery store and do errands, weeding, and yard work. I've gained about five pounds but still have at least ten more to go.

The boys are back here every day. I can take Mikey outside again for adventures, even if we don't go quite as far. Annette does the vast majority of their care, but I can help out. Annette is my rock, my hero! Without her I would not have been able to get through this.

Randy Thorp is a sixty-eight year old retired librarian and COVID survivor. He and his partner, Annette Merritt, help care for her young grandsons while their parents work.

A NURSE'S PERSPECTIVE

» **BY DEBBIE BOADA**

When I reflect on the start of 2020, there were so many exciting things that were going to happen. There were going to be the usual holiday and birthday celebrations, but there were also going to be many firsts this year.

There was rumbling in the background about a virus. I had heard of other viruses in other countries throughout my years in the medical field as a nurse. Fortunately for the United States, many never fully made it here. I wasn't worried.

My son-in-law graduated from Kennesaw State University in December with a Masters degree that was potentially going to take him out of the country. Exciting, yes, and a very proud accomplishment. My daughter was expecting their first child, who was due in late July. My brother was expecting his first grandchild, due in March, and made the decision to move closer to his daughter in Orlando. This made me very happy for our family. My brother and I would be closer and going on to enjoy the next phase of our lives. I fortunately had two grandchildren already, from my son and daughter-in-law.

My great nephew was born in early March and I was able to meet him on his second day of life. Hospital protocols had not changed yet, but COVID-19 was in the US and it was about to change all our lives. New York was spiraling out of control with cases. I was still optimistic it would not spread. They would control it in New York. About one week later, the country started to lock down.

I had not been to a grocery store in a few weeks and was dumbfounded as to why there was no toilet paper. Why?

My health is pretty good except for the many extra pounds I drag around. I frequently develop a pretty awful-sounding cough that startles people who don't know me. Protocols were changing at work, but COVID-19 numbers in Gainesville were low. My cough was increasing, and I was out of my usual inhalers. My husband grew concerned as my cough worsened, and one night he was very worried and insisted I go to the emergency room. Protocols had now changed. He wasn't allowed in the room with me. Doctors and nurses were more cautious as they approached me. I was confident all I needed was my inhalers. They insisted on doing a full cardiac workup to make sure I wasn't having a heart attack. I didn't meet the algorithm to get tested for the virus. In the end, my heart was fine, and I got my inhalers. I went back to work on Monday. My coughing was awful, and I raised a few eyebrows, but they knew me, and I have coughed like this before.

Wednesday of that week I developed a fever. There were not any in-person doctor visits, so I saw my doctor online. Now, that was weird. She was concerned, and I was stressed out. I now met the algorithm to get tested. My head was spinning with how many people

I had been in contact with. I had worked on the children's oncology unit that Monday. I was a total wreck thinking about the harm I might have done.

Saturday morning, my test came back negative. What a relief! I continued coughing for a few weeks, and I wasn't allowed to go back to work. I was treated with two rounds of steroids and antibiotics and finally felt better.

Now I was ready to go back to work. I had used up all my sick and vacation leave and, like a lot of people, I needed to get back to work. School was online. Restaurants, bars, theatres were all closed. People were dying. Protocols at work had changed drastically. People couldn't have visitors. All elective surgery had been canceled. Doctor visits were online. Gainesville numbers were up, and adults were being admitted very sick. Children were not.

I have been a pediatric nurse for thirty years. Children were not getting COVID-19, thank goodness. Since children were at home, they were also not getting sick or hurt. I am not hoping for children to be sick or hurt, but it meant that pediatric nurses were unable to work. The hospital began to find other ways for us to work. Contact tracing jobs and doing temperature checks and COVID testing have become a new normal. Children are active again. They are returning to school and playing and contracting the COVID-19. They probably were getting it months ago but were not tested.

In Gainesville, we have been lucky with our children not getting critically ill with the virus. The concern for me is, will this virus cause them any problems later in life? The not-knowing lives in the back of my mind. I have been in contact with COVID positive children at work. I wear my personal protection equipment, otherwise known as PPE. PPE remains a problem. I wear my homemade mask every time I go out.

I am proud of most Gainesville residents and businesses. We have a city mandate to wear a mask. Such an easy thing to do, yet there is division. When I think of my cancer families or any family with chronic illness and the sacrifices they make, I am in awe. I get very angry at people who complain about not being able to live their lives or having to wear a mask—a small sacrifice we have to make to limit the transmission of this potentially dangerous virus.

Debbie Boada is a Certified Pediatric Registered Nurse who has been working as a pediatric nurse since 1989. Born in Brooklyn, NY to Cuban immigrant parents, she grew up in Miami, FL. To raise her children in a less hectic environment, she moved to Gainesville, FL. She works at Shands as a "float nurse," basically working in any pediatric unit that needs a nurse for that shift. This gives her a diverse experience in caring for children. She loves to sew for her grandchildren, tries to stay involved with her Temple life, and in better times volunteered in local charities.

(PHOTO BY CONNIE DOBY)

THE GLADYS BERTHA SIMMONS STORY

THE IMPACT OF COVID-19 ON HER LIFE & DEATH

» **BY CAROLYN BROWN SPOONER**

My aunt, Mrs. Gladys B. Simmons, age eighty-six, was admitted to a rehab center on June 10, 2020. She tested negative for COVID-19 prior to and upon admission, but was quarantined for two weeks as part of the facility's COVID protocol. She was not allowed visitors and could only speak with her family via phone. I was told she would be transferred to a new unit after the two week quarantine period and would have a treatment team consisting of a doctor, nurse, rehab staff, dietitian, and social worker. The team would hold regular meetings and advise me on her progress. The goal was for her to get stronger and return home to live independently.

(PHOTO BY CAROLYN BROWN SPOONER)

She began to make very good progress and was getting ready to go home in July. Suddenly, around the 3rd week of July, she called and said she needed to see me. I asked what was wrong. She said, "I just don't feel well." I asked the staff what was going on. The staff member stated she had been doing very well, but that day she was dragging her left leg and couldn't do her exercises. I asked had she reported this to the doctor and nurse to ensure my aunt had not suffered a stroke. She replied she would report it to the nurse.

I followed up later that afternoon with the on duty nurse, who informed me no one had told her about this and there was nothing in the chart. I was shocked. The nurse said she would follow up on the matter.

After several days, the nurse said my aunt was doing fine. I visited the facility on July 31st and asked to see her through the window, but was told she was resting and didn't feel like getting up. Had she been examined for possible stroke? The nurse didn't know but would follow up with the doctor. I called to speak with the facility administrators and left several messages with them and the nurse, but to no avail. There were no return calls.

August 8th, I received a call that my aunt had tested positive and was being moved to their COVID unit. I spoke with the nurse on duty who stated she was new to the unit and didn't know much about what they did. They were not providing COVID treatment since my aunt had no symptoms. What did she call loss of appetite and not being able to function well for two weeks? She stated Mrs. Simmons had eaten her meal and was presenting no COVID symptoms. When I asked to speak with my aunt, it was not allowed because there could be droplets on the phone.

After several frustrating days I demanded to speak with the facility administrator. Eight days later, he called and apologized for not getting back to me. I told him I had been trying for weeks to get someone to let me know my aunt's status, whether she had been examined for stroke, or if she needed to go to a hospital. He assured me he would look into the matter and arrange a team meeting within the week.

The meeting was August 18th. They said my aunt was doing okay. I asked if she was eating, and the dietician said she was eating less than fifty percent. Were they giving her the appetite stimulant, Megestrol? The nurse said, no, the doctor hadn't written a prescription for it yet. I was told she weighed 120 pounds. She had lost over twenty pounds.

They said she tested negative for COVID and if she continued to test negative, they would move her back to a regular unit. The nurse didn't know what medications my aunt was taking and didn't have the medication list at hand. She said she'd get the list and let me know. Also, the doctor would call me regarding the appetite stimulant, but neither called. I couldn't speak with my aunt during the meeting because she had fallen asleep. She shouldn't have been asleep at that time of day, nor in the middle of the meeting.

I asked about their plan. The team stated they would write up a treatment plan to encourage eating. They assured me she didn't need to go to the hospital. Twelve hours later, however, I got a call, saying my aunt was being admitted to the hospital for abnormal labs. Within a few hours, the ER called stating my aunt was being moved to ICU, that her condition was grave. Her vital organs were shutting down and she was being intubated. She was found to be suffering from sepsis from a urinary tract infection.

My heart dropped. I told the doctor I had been trying for weeks to get the rehab center to evaluate my aunt, but each time they told me she was doing fine and she didn't need to go to the hospital. The doctor said they got her there a little too late to do her any good. She had suffered multiple strokes and her vital organs were shutting down. She was dying.

"Lord have mercy!" I thought. How painfully hurt and angry did I feel, knowing the rehab center had neglected her under the cloak of COVID-19 protocol! My aunt, Gladys Simmons, died as a result of neglect, suffering from sepsis, multiple strokes, and starvation due to protocol preventing her from being seen by family. COVID-19 gives power to nursing homes and rehab centers to lock patients away from their families, leaving them to die.

My aunt went from looking healthy in June 2020, able to touch her toes at eighty-six, to being dead on August 24, 2020.

Covid-19 gives facilities a cloak of protection to neglect their patients, leaving them to die without proper care.

This is the Gladys Bertha Simmons' story, and I hope no one else ever has to go through this dreadful experience.

Carolyn Brown Spooner is a native of Bradford County, the daughter of the late Willie and Louiza Brown of Starke. She graduated from Bradford High School in 1970; Bethune-Cookman College, 1974, B.S. Psychology; and the University of Florida in 1975, M.Ed. and Ed.S. Counselor Education. She was nominated for the Florida Times Union EVE Award and was honored by TV 20 as a Community Builder. She is a poet, song writer, and children's book author who has received song copyrights for "Drunk Driver Get Off the Road" and "I'm So Sick of Your Saggy Pants." Her recent children's book is *Peggy the Slow Poke Train*.

IN PRISON WITH COVID

» BY SALLY WILSON

For the last five years, I have felt so isolated from the rest of the world...I reside in prison—merely twenty-six miles from my Gainesville home, but a world away. I am incarcerated at Lowell Annex, located in Ocala, Florida, part of the largest women's prison in the country, separated from my loved ones, my every move controlled.

As news of the pandemic became the lead story on every news show in early March, my eighty-six dorm mates and I wondered how it would affect us. Although I am able bodied, I live in the elderly/ADA dorm among many older women with underlying conditions. We thought, isolated as we are from the outside world, we would either be totally safe, or be sitting ducks!

The first restriction was the loss of visits from family and friends. I was one of the lucky few to have my birthday visit that last weekend. The decision to suspend visits came quickly. Within a week of losing visits, volunteers were no longer allowed, classes and religious services ended. Our movement inside the prison became even more controlled. Our usual activities were halted. We were only allowed to be with others from our dorm, no casual stroll to the chow hall, no leaving the dorm for our work assignments, no mixing with the other 1000 plus women here. We were told all these were temporary measures, and as the President wrongly informed the nation, we were also told everything would be back to normal by Easter.

Next came the masks, the social distancing, and only essential workers were allowed out of our dorms. We were constantly assured—no COVID cases here. Then word came. It was in other prisons...and then it was here! I tested positive! No breathing problems, but the fatigue was like nothing I'd felt before. My bunky, (or bunkmate, the gal in the bed only eighteen inches away), and I would lie in our beds and just stare at each other. We took turns resting and getting each other's meals.

Meals were delivered, but with no inmate labor to cook, we were given bologna or peanut butter sandwiches for days on end.

Guards began to realize the magnitude of the essential work done by "inmate labor." The education staff slapped bologna on a Styrofoam tray, scooped peanut butter from five-gallon buckets. The guards washed our laundry, mowed the grounds, and delivered meals and other items, like the all-important toilet paper.

As our loved ones lost their income, the flow of money into the prison slowed, but we can't go to the inmate store anyway. Contrary to popular belief, not "everything" is provided in prison. Shampoo, deodorant, and lotion starts to run short, then the supply of instant coffee I buy in the commissary runs out. Like the other inmates, I survive on instant coffee and Ramen noodle soups. But weeks went by with no shopping. The supply of coffee I kept in my drawer is all gone! I am an avid coffee drinker. Eventually, I was able to replenish my coffee supply but not the cream or sugar. I must drink my coffee black, but having lost my senses of taste and smell, I don't even miss the cream and sugar.

We went weeks without seeing daylight. Inmates were removed via stretcher and we never knew where they went. And then the first confirmed death from our dorm, a seventy-five year old woman, in great health, but dead in ten days time. She slept four beds away from me!

Eventually, nearly everyone tested positive, there was no one else to infect, so the virus ran its course. We are still separated from other dorms, but things slowly return to the new normal. Now we wait for a second wave, or a vaccine.

You who live outside the prison gates now share my existence, trapped in your homes as I am behind prison walls. You are not free to go out to eat, free to shop, free to attend religious services as you formerly did! How strange for you, but just another day in lock-down for me.

You are still free to resist no matter how foolish those actions are. No solitary confinement for you, should you hug a friend or not wear your mask. You are free to choose to risk it all by attending an event. I remain behind locked doors. Am I safer? I guess not, as I see them wheel away another inmate who will not return from the infirmary...our first confirmed COVID-19 death.

The Visitors Area has been turned into an overflow infirmary, port-a-potties and portable showers out in the yard. We watch TV—you had the temporary hospitals going up, and now we have one of our own.

Newscasters talk of the sick being all alone, dying without loved ones near, but that is how it always is for a dying inmate, except that an inmate is cuffed to the bed until they take their dying breath. And now the world can't have funerals, just like us. There is never a memorial service in prison.

Just like the guards here, you who live outside these gates and who rely on the services of others suddenly start to appreciate the essential workers, the store clerks, and the delivery drivers.

As we spend more and more time locked down, the pettiness and arguments increase. Is it any different than the cooped-up college kids forced back to Mom and Dad's house?

Finally, we are allowed out for thirty minutes of fresh air...we emerge like zombies...

Everyone is feeling better, but still the restrictions continue. The guards become complacent, the PPEs are carried rather than worn. They get tired of constantly yelling at us to wear our masks properly, as they wear theirs around their arms. The guards' numbers are diminished, and they work so much overtime, they seem to be "doing" time along with us. For once, the outside world suffers the same restrictions as do we...maybe we aren't so different after all.

Sally Wilson has called Alachua County home since 1972, but for the past six years she has lived in Marion County as an inmate at Lowell Correctional Institution, the country's largest women's prison. Her "free" world career was in real estate, but in prison she works in the law library, helping other inmates with their legal issues. She has a few more years of incarceration and then plans to return to her friends and family in the Gainesville area. She is always eager to correspond with anyone interested in the lives of women in prison.

PUNCHING BAG CLOWN

» **BY JAMES W. HARPER**

Blow up the plastic clown
A punching bag for children
Watch it wobble
As small hands deliver blows.
Knock it down, clown pops back up
Push it over, it pops right back.

Now I have become a hollow COVID clown
Infected by an invisible enemy
Knocking me down, pushing me over.

Round 1: Sneak attack
At a family's dinner table
Stabbed by a microscopic fork
Never seen, never felt

Round 2: The fever strikes
The migraine flashes—
Direct jabs to my mouth
Forcing toxic spittle to fly

Round 3: Stumble forward
Evade the swirling plastic gloves
Grab the chicken soup
From Wah Ha Ha Thai Food Restaurant

Round 4: The prize fighter
Turns away from me
Towards my love
Delivering blow after blow

Round 5: The neon yellow ambulance
Arrives to take my love away—
The knockout punch

Deflated, I melt onto the front porch steps.
Beyond the asphalt, an old woman
Presses her palm
Against a screen door.

James W. Harper works in communications at the University of Florida in Gainesville. He spent 10 years as an environmental journalist in Miami, published more than 300 articles, and wrote an eco-memoir, *Passion Fruit.* He has been an English teacher abroad and at various levels in the U.S. He raises backyard chickens and is an All-American swimmer.

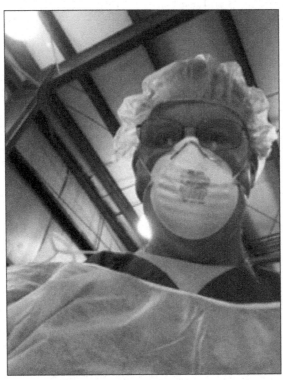

(PHOTO BY DAVID WILLIAMS)

"I volunteered to help my community at a time in need. I was just one of the many volunteers that helped. We tested four people every seven minutes or at least that was how they were scheduled."

– David Williams, Registered Nurse

HEALTH, JUSTICE, AND COVID-19

» **BY ROBIN LEWY, KAELI FLANNERY, AND FRAN RICARDO**

The Rural Women's Health Project (RWHP) was established in 1991 as a non-profit based in Gainesville, serving North Central Florida. Its mission is to build community programs and policies that strengthen communities' capacity to overcome health and social justice barriers through leadership development, advocacy, coalition-building, and health linkages.

Health justice is the fusion of access to medical care and social support and one's power over their own health and body. It is a right, in tune with the socio-economic, multicultural, and multilingual realities of our communities. Health justice makes health achievable for the individual and society.

The onset of COVID-19 exposed the need for culturally relevant health information and services to diverse communities. A disproportionate burden of poor health outcomes and deaths from the pandemic fell on the backs of people of color, rural populations, and those with chronic health conditions. A reliable, justice-driven response to these inequities required action, adaptability, and collaboration, often outside of public systems.

Government agencies have not prioritized equitable, language-inclusive health information. Critical factors, such as health literacy and the digital divide, are vastly underestimated. Prevention and management messages disregard cultural, social, and economic barriers. Health disparities are exacerbated by failure to address limited English-proficiency and a historical distrust of government entities.

Latino immigrants, in particular, have faced disproportionate challenges. Accounting for a large share of frontline essential workers, they endure greater health risks than the general population. In Alachua County, this includes labor in agriculture, hospitality, and health services.

Early in the pandemic, the RWHP scrambled to deliver information to Latino immigrants, using community-embedded social networks and mobile messaging in Spanish and Mayan languages throughout North Central Florida, to provide links to medical and social services via trusted sources.

Decoding scientific messaging was the first step. We relied on our team of Latino community members and health professionals for input to revise our COVID-19 *Consejos* (Advice), one-page visual tip sheets in Spanish, designed to teach self-identification of health risks. Each message provides realistic options for prevention and self-care.

We adapted our traditional *Promotores de Salud* (Community Health Worker) model into a *Comunicadoras* model. *Comunicadoras* are a group of community leaders who disseminate Spanish and Mam language messages to a circle of their friends, coworkers, and family through phone calls or text messages. This emphasizes social distancing rather than face-to-face communication, and uses familiar methods to deliver trusted, medically sound, culturally-appropriate information to immigrant communities, while also creating a bridge to potentially needed services and resources.

Messages provided critical and consistent information on COVID-19 prevention, government orders on lockdowns, mask use, testing locations, etc., and provided timely updates, as information rapidly changed. Since April, 2020, the *Consejo* Program has delivered thousands of messages through ten *Comunicadoras* and thirteen Latino-serving partner agencies in three counties and continues to inform community members about vaccines, new ordinances, and prevention recommendations. The *Consejos,* including video formats and PSAs, are available in Spanish, Mam, and Mixteco and are used across the U.S. by immigrant-serving agencies.

As non-English speaking Latinos began testing positive for COVID-19 or were hospitalized, it became evident that local government and health systems were unprepared to serve this community. Frequent calls to our office reflected agencies' impatience in the "lack of compliance of Latino community members" in following prevention recommendations and assisting contact tracers. However, no prior efforts had been made to ensure the participation of non-English speakers through education and outreach. This historical indifference to the growing Latino population meant that distrust, negative assumptions, and disconnect persisted between these agencies and the Latino community. Paramount concern was the lack of inclusive planning or activated language lines or certified multilingual staff to handle concerned community members' calls.

As COVID-19 hit a peak in early summer, North Central Florida agencies had no plan on how to serve the influx of agricultural workers in the blueberry and watermelon harvests. When COVID-19 testing was done on a work crew, and 90 of 100 workers tested positive, it was clear that the lack of preparation would result in disproportionate and deadly outcomes. At least one farmworker in our area died in farmworker housing from COVID-19. Others who were sick were told to keep working and to quarantine at night. The disregard for the wellbeing of this community and the unjust approach to serving monolingual Spanish speakers, who are the labor behind our region's agricultural profits, reflects our painful area history. This neglect moved us to develop *Best Practices for*

COVID-19 Response in Rural Farmworker Populations, an infographic brief for health departments. Our intent was to inform them of the nuances of farmworker realities and offer recommendations to justly serve them during COVID.

Additionally, the RWHP volunteered to provide COVID-19 testing to farmworkers on location, assisting the health department. Our advocacy to city and county officials for health services and food distribution for workers was met with mixed results, leaving us to find other agencies and volunteers to offer hygiene products and legal advice on labor rights, including the right to seek emergency medical care.

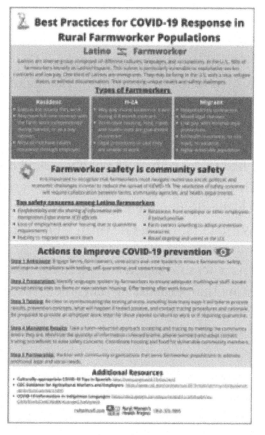

We enlisted trusted churches and agencies to provide the location and framework for testing the broader Latino community. We then partnered with health departments, medical reserve programs, and medical students through the Community Medicine program at the University of Florida. This provided one-stop opportunities to provide the Latino community with health education, masks, and testing by Spanish-speaking health workers. These efforts, combined with advocacy for accessible Spanish-language assistance on health department COVID-19 phone lines, moderated distrust and increased Latino participation in COVID-19 response efforts.

The broad diversity of Latino immigrants in our region face immense and disproportionate challenges during the pandemic. Without access to timely, accurate, high-quality information and services, health disparities will continue to surge for Latino communities. At the RWHP, we hope to continue to dismantle distrust, build understanding, and place Latinos at the forefront of efforts to mitigate inequitable health and economic outcomes from COVID-19 and future health crises.

Robin Lewy, MA, Kaeli Flannery, MPH, and Fran Ricardo, BS, are team members at the Rural Women's Health Project. Established in 1991, the RWHP's mission is to use evidence-based strategies to build sustainable and replicable community programs and policies to strengthen communities' capacity to overcome health and social justice barriers, by involving them in the development and implementation of research findings. They seek to build the capacity of emerging leaders, create advocacy opportunities, build coalition, and improve linkage to health protective services.

THE MEDICAL PERSPECTIVE

» **BY J. NISHIDA**

Poem 1

"Remember that patient, intubated?" – I do remember him
A fifty-something, healthy – tiring out just breathing
"Well, he didn't make it" – My heart sinks, I wonder
Are other patients at home dying? When they should be seeing a doctor?

I had to put him on the phone – And hold it to her ear
He told her he loved her so – I wipe away her tears
The hardest moment seeing – Helpless patients die
Without family beside them – Or over an iPad, a COVID patient says goodbye

His wife, she begged and pleaded – Staff can't bend no-visit rules
More than exhausting schedule – Was witnessing the toll
On patients and on families – It really hits home
Absence of patients' families – Can't see your loved one and then they're gone

I'm used to treating patients – No one afraid of treating the sick
It's very different knowing – The patient is actually a risk
Fellow healthcare providers – When they start getting sick
It's hardest, it's really scary – Who is going to take care of the public?

Nighttime is the hardest – You're constantly thinking
The fear that lives within us – What will the next day bring?
The nurses and the doctors – The more than 12-hour shift
It's frustrating and scary – Just not knowing what comes next

COVID-19 has affected – A lot of people's lives
Converge and join the platform – I ask all people worldwide
Nobody can fight individually – Colleagues, loved ones at home
We've come together in a crisis – I think that's what is giving me hope

Poem 2

I lied to mom, she let me – The woman reads my mind
I'm low risk, I'm not worried – (I've jinxed myself?) I'm fine
I lie to a lot of patients – It's going to be okay
But COVID is a trickster – It manifests in a myriad of ways

Evolving, another nightmare – Feel helpless, surreal pain
Passover, rabbi praying – Unleavened bread, wine, plague
My mask, the ugly bruise marks – The dearth of PPE
"Es felt mir vi a lokh in kop" – My grandmother would sigh

Younger, healthier patients – Overcome in ICU
A withering of the spirit – Away floating balloon
"No emergencies in a pandemic" – Don't rush, affix your own mask
But when light in the eyes snuffs out – It's difficult to think, not simply react

The number of ventilators – The mathematics, it's grim
The epicenter of a pandemic – Our missteps, we're blind men
But we're talking to one another – I want to be learned from
We treat patients we will never see – In telling patients' courses and outcomes

My boyfriend reads before bed – To me to quiet my mind
Books, stories have always been – My dress rehearsal for life
"I wish it need not have happened," said Frodo, "In my time"
"And so do all who…see such times. But that is not for them to decide"

J. Nishida, sometimes host of Gainesville's Thursday Night Poetry Jam, has been a student of science, education, language, linguistics, and literature, and has worked as an English teacher, library story lady, mom, and with nonprofits supporting arts and education. She has had poems published in the 2019 & 2020 *Bacopa Literary Review* and is currently editing a book of Japanese waka poetry translations.

THIS CAR WRECK OF A YEAR

» **BY WENDY THORNTON**

Recently, I had a long list of errands to run and started towards my car, but my husband, Ken, stopped me on the way out the door. He wanted me to see the amazing work he'd done in the yard. Now, I'm one of those obsessive people who makes constant lists and always worry I won't complete every item on the list. I needed to get going. But that day, I stopped to see what he had done in the back yard.

At the beginning of the pandemic, we'd had a bunch of old, decrepit trees taken down. Over the course of the past few months, Ken worked on the yard, pulling up weeds, putting down mulch, turning it into a beautiful sanctuary. I was in a hurry to get all the errands done, but I just had to sit for a few moments and admire the beautiful view. Finally, you could see the blue sky. Finally, we had green grass rather than a jungle of invasives. Finally, we had a beautiful yard. We sat at our outdoor table underneath an umbrella and admired the spectacular day.

Suddenly, we heard a crash. And then another! Whatever had just happened, it sounded very close.

I jumped up and went down to the end of the street to see what was going on. My neighbors told me that a young kid had hit and killed a deer at the end of our street, and then a young girl had crashed *her* car into his.

Now, let me explain something—I live in the middle of suburbia. Deer do not run rampant in this area. Wild deer have never explored our manicured, fenced-in backyard. I'll bet the kid was driving too fast—it seems these days that everyone drives too fast—but he could hardly have expected to hit a deer in the middle of the road outside Suburban Heights.

We could see him pacing up and down beside the dead deer, while the young girl who hit him from behind was frantically yelling into her cell phone.

Ironically, I related to how they felt. In February, 2020, before the pandemic, I was on my way to teach a class at Santa Fe College when a teenager made a U-turn on this very same road and crashed into my almost new van. No one was hurt, but I was devastated. I missed my last class of the winter session and my vehicle was wiped out and had to be towed. The kid who hit me actually cried, and his parents came to pick him up. I felt so sorry for him, but I was also crushed, because my husband and I had planned to use that van to travel out west in the summer of 2020. We were going to Colorado, Arizona, Wyoming, and most especially, to Utah. My husband, an artist, wanted to capture on canvas the beautiful rocks and mountains of the west. He and I were planning to spend a month meandering through national parks and travelling along scenic highways.

The best laid plans, right? Ken had gone out west the year before by himself, and he'd painted dozens of amazing pictures, which got him accepted into the Spring Arts Festival for 2020. You know, the one that was cancelled.

Let's back up. This year has been stunningly eventful for us. First, there was my wreck. Then, a few weeks later, Ken had a mild stroke. This meant that I became the driver of the family, the errand runner, the organizer. And then came the cascade of events—my spring classes at Santa Fe were cancelled, my writing meetings were cancelled, Ken's first ever Spring Arts Festival appearance was cancelled, our trip out west was cancelled. We ended up home-schooling our grandkids from March to June, and then, in July, we caught the COVID virus. Folks, believe me, it ain't the flu! We were incapacitated for weeks.

Now, here's the deal. You'd think with all these things going on, that I would be depressed and want to run off screaming into the night. And there are certainly times when I feel overwhelmed by all the bad vibes 2020 has brought our way. Sometimes I feel like we're living in the Twilight Zone.

But then, there are these weird, beautiful things that have happened. My van now runs better than before. My husband's cognitive function improves daily. When I was sick, I became really close to my neighbors, who provided us with food, gifts, and deserts while we were recovering from the evil virus. I learned to use Publix Instacart. And I'm getting really good at home-schooling my grandkids.

But the big thing is this—I have learned to appreciate the things that previously might have passed me by. My husband, who has never been the least bit interested in yard work, has become a virtual *phytologist*, a plant expert. He grows stronger every day. And our yard has become more of an oasis where we can hang out with our grandkids, visit with our neighbors in a social distanced environment, and play with the new puppies we adopted to help us through the pandemic.

This year began with a horrendous accident which could have been much worse. I'm glad I wasn't hurt, and the kid who hit me wasn't hurt. But if I hadn't stopped, literally on my way out the door, to admire the beautiful yard work of my recovering husband, I could have been involved in that accident half a block away. Maybe I wouldn't have hit the deer, and maybe the two kids in the wreck wouldn't have hit me. But you never know.

Who could guess that the beauty of wind blowing through the trees backed by a deep blue sky would cause someone, who is an obsessively list-oriented compulsive organizer, to stop for just the few moments needed to be safe? Onward, 2020!

Wendy Thornton has been published in *Riverteeth, Epiphany, MacGuffin* and many other literary journals. Her book of music essays, *Sounding the Depths*, was published in May 2018. Her latest Bear Trapped mystery, *Bear Trapped: Blowback* was published in 2019. Her memoir, *Dear Oprah: How I Beat Cancer and Learned to Love Daytime TV*, was published in 2013. She teaches writing courses at Santa Fe College. She was also nominated for a Pushcart Prize, has won many literary awards, and started the Writers Alliance (www.writersalliance.org). Besides her U.S. publications, her writing has appeared in England, Ireland, Australia, and India.

VULNERABLE TIMES

» BY ANDREA VILLA RUIZ

So, it hit me… not while I was panicking, no. During those couple of minutes my heart was galloping, legs trembling, hands in a shaky despair. It happened a few minutes after the stranger stopped banging on my door, uninvited, unannounced. Luna was quick to respond with a loud and constant bark, but the man did not like it and continued to knock on my door even louder. I was able to get a glimpse of his silhouette from my window upstairs, but he looked up, too, and saw me hiding behind the blinds and continued to knock. I felt vulnerable.

By this time the panic grew exponentially and all I could think about doing was to call a close friend who lives nearby. His quick response overwhelmed me with gratefulness and in less than seven minutes he said he could see the man knocking on other doors a few apartments away from mine. It was then that it hit me, right at that moment, communicating with my friend via phone while he was seated in his car outside. We are in strict quarantine and practicing social distance. We have not seen each other in weeks. Yet, the threat tonight was not the COVID-19 virus itself.

Tonight, for the first time in weeks I felt fear unrelated to the virus and its lethal consequences. Perhaps, it is worth mentioning that a few days ago that same friend who came to the social-distance style rescue had already warned me that something like that had happened to him and to his neighbors. He called immediately to tell me about the incident, to urge me not to take Luna for a walk at night, to find ways to ensure my safety at home during these unfathomable times.

Today, his episode and my episode played in my mind repeatedly while I was finding resourceful ways to block my doors in hopes of having a peaceful night's sleep. A night in which isolation and the ephemeral glimpse of my friend sitting in his car outside were the only two companions Luna and I had. The virus is having consequences that we might not even visualize yet; consequences that can be as harmful and as terrifying as the virus itself.

Andrea Villa Ruiz was born and raised in Bogotá, Colombia. She is currently a Lecturer in Spanish at the University of Florida. She holds a BA in International Studies (Loras College, 2004) and master's degrees in Latin American Studies and Spanish Literature (University of South Florida, 2008, 2010). She has a Ph.D. in Spanish from the University of Florida (2016). When Andrea is not working she is walking with Luna–her adorable schnauzer–or doing virtual Pilates with her friends.

CHAPTER 3

THE NEW NORMAL

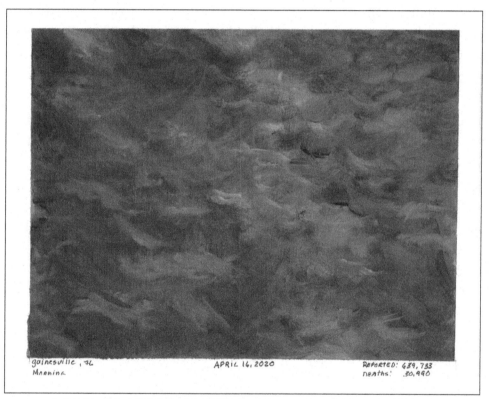

gainesville, FL
Morning
APRIL 16, 2020
REPORTED: 639,733
Deaths: 30,990

APRIL 16, 2020 (GWENDOLYN CHRZANOWSKI)

HOW THE COVID-19 PANDEMIC HAS CHANGED MY LIFE

» **BY JOAN H. CARTER**

Fortunately, I'm retired, so I didn't have a job to be disrupted by the COVID-19 pandemic. I have fewer personal contacts now, while my already busy email life has expanded. Scheduled activities continue online, courtesy of Zoom. Thank goodness for Zoom! It's not perfect, but we can see and hear each other, in some ways even better than during in-person meetings. But I used to carpool with a friend to meetings, and I miss the chats we had on the way. In seven months, I've had only three lunches with a friend. I see more neighbors walking past the house, which is nice, but rather than stopping to chat as they used to, they are more apt to keep walking. My weekly tai chi class hasn't met; perhaps that's why my walking isn't as steady as it was.

An ominous air of danger enwraps the community. I've noticed some people wearing a mask don't even look at others, acting as if a smile or a wave to a stranger can make them sick. Little old ladies like me are especially vulnerable to the scary virus, so I'm less apt to venture out to do errands. I wear a mask when I go to the store or the doctor, and I wash my hands after every venture outside. For doctor visits, I have to pass a temperature check and assert that, "No, I haven't lost my sense of smell," "I don't have a headache," and "I feel fine."

I head to Publix early in the morning, before I'm really awake, when few others are there and the air in the store is fresher. Instead of shopping when I'm about to run out of something, I'm going only weekly now, which means planning ahead. I must guess whether I have enough milk, bread, and strawberries to last a whole week. Unusual store outages require adaptation. When Publix was out of creamy peanut butter, I bought chunky. Not liking lumps in food, I had avoided it for years, but I learned I like chunky peanut butter after all!

My days have changed. I'm spending way too much time online. After breakfast, I start my day on email, to get it out of the way, I tell myself. My immediate family has agreed to a daily round robin email to check on each other during these threatening times. Usually I start the conversation, since I'm in the Eastern Time Zone, and the others are on Pacific Time. As I connect to the internet, something called "Pocket" pops up—I think Google sends it—with a list of fascinating articles to read, and I'll see emailed news from *The Week*, a printed magazine to which I subscribe. Maybe I'll add a comment to my family note about one of those news items, I think. I used to read an article or two from Pocket and all the news from *The Week* before writing my email.

Daily "Coronavirus Updates" began coming from the *Washington Post*. I started tracking the daily counts of new cases and deaths, especially those for Alachua County and

Gainesville, but I've given that up. The daily numbers go up and down. Mostly up. They don't tell me whether I'm in danger in my neighborhood. It's the same discouraging news every day about the rest of the country, just bigger numbers.

Then other newsy emails started coming from everywhere. Now CNN and the *New York Times* are the earliest to greet me. The *Washington Post* follows. And Apple News. Throughout the day, the *New York Times* sends "Breaking News" headlines, and the *Washington Post* sends more "Coronavirus Updates." I hear from the *Los Angeles Times* and get special editorials from its Politico.com editor. Sometimes, *The Atlantic* or the *Guardian* sends a treasure to read. The *National Geographic* has joined the crowd.

I've learned I can spend all morning just browsing those articles and the links in them. So, I just read one or two now before inputting to the round robin. Usually. Unless I just can't resist wondering what's behind another title, or what's in the other emails that have come in.

Besides reading those articles and contributing to the family email, I may receive a link from my brother to an article he's read in his newspaper, either a news event or a political treatise. He's interested in my feedback, so of course I read it and respond. He also includes me in some of his email discussions with his friends about current issues, so I read those conversations and sometimes offer my two cents.

I keep telling myself I must quit reading all that stuff and get some work done. But there is so much going on now! I find myself often spending all afternoon into the night reading what's in my inbox and still can't read it all. Then with supper, I read the local printed newspaper. Afterwards, it's the comics and working the puzzles in the paper to clear my head for sleep.

How did a faithful newspaper reader turn into a person who only reads the paper for the smattering of local news and commentary, comics, and Sudoku puzzles? After the election, will the draw of the internet taper off? We'll still have the coronavirus, severe economic problems, racial and political tensions, and probably severe weather disasters. I will still see those interesting accounts of history or other topics that tempt me to read. But maybe politics and riots will calm down. And next spring, maybe virus outbreaks and shutdowns will lessen, too. Perhaps then I can wean myself off news long enough to get some of my to-do projects done.

Meanwhile, I am up to date on the big issues facing our country. I've learned the internet is a fantastic source of current events information. And I'm keeping a jar of delicious chunky peanut butter in the cupboard.

Joan Carter lives alone in a large house full of keepsakes that help her remember details for the memoirs she writes, but that she needs to get rid of so she can move to simpler quarters. She's working on a trilogy of memoirs to document the multiple lives she's led.

MY TWO CENTS ON THE CORONAVIRUS

» BY CONNIE BIDDLE MORRISON

The restrictions caused by the pandemic have not changed things all that significantly for me. Some things have been improved, but a few have been difficult to deal with. I am a homebody to begin with, so gallivanting out and about has never been high on my list of daily activities. I am perfectly happy to stay at home most of the time.

Not having visitors, though, has been tough, especially family members. Just before the pandemic got into full gear, one of my granddaughters announced that she was expecting her second child with a due date in September. I envisioned lots of get-togethers, including a baby shower, and then being at the hospital just after the birth as I was with their first baby.

None of this was to be. Gifts were sent by UPS and communication was limited to text messages and photos. Then, on the morning of September 12th, I texted my granddaughter to see how she was doing. Her due date had been set for September 9th and everyone was getting antsy. She texted back that she was just leaving for a walk to try to encourage the start of labor. I replied, "That should do it."

And it did. At 2:27 in the afternoon, Hubby sent a photo of them with thumbs up, in the car and on the way to the hospital. At 3:39, Colt Arthur was born, 21 ½" long and weighing 8 pounds and 6 ounces. Only Hubby was allowed in the room. But text messages and photos were flying across the airwaves, very different from the birth of my first great-grandchild, but wonderful all the same.

The worst thing is not being able to hold the little one in my arms, feeling his tiny fingers wrapping around mine, smelling his new baby smell, feeling the heft of him, hearing his cry and gurgles, looking into his eyes and seeing the beginning of a smile form for the first time. These are the things I miss the most. I struggle with the overpowering urge to throw caution to the wind.

Good things that are the result of the coronavirus include meetings on Zoom. No more is it necessary to travel for group discussions on things of interest. No gasoline to buy, no rainy weather to worry about, and no dressing up in finery (I did not do that anyway). I would not mind too much if Zoom meetings continued forever. But I cannot get used to not seeing friends and family in person.

Another good thing is the time I now have to finish all those partially-completed projects, although many continue to hang around, leaving me feeling guilty. I have finished a children's book and on September 25th, I shall have a proof to edit. This has been my biggest surprise, since I have been working on a memoir forever and never considered writing a children's book as a viable goal for myself. To have written it and completed the self-publishing process (so far) on my own has done wonders for my self-confidence.

Although I consider wearing a mask mandatory for any absolutely necessary excursions, I find it confining and unpleasant. My glasses fog and my normally soft voice goes unheard completely, in many instances causing some stress. But, as I have noted from somewhere, you can get used to anything. Maybe, maybe not. There are some things I do not want to get used to and mask-wearing is one of them.

Connie Biddle Morrison grew up in Delaware, near the eastern shore, and spent her childhood delighting in the smell of salty marshes. She writes creative non-fiction short stories about her younger years and the role of the Delaware marshlands in her life. Her stories have been published in *Long Story Short, All Things Girl, Senior Times* magazines, and *Chicken Soup for the Soul*. She lives near Gainesville, Florida.

(PHOTO BY PASTOR KARL ANDERSON)

Cars in line at the Oaks Mall in Gainesville, Florida, on April 20, 2020. In response to food insecurity in the region, the Alachua County Christian Pastors Association created Community Relief Days to provide food to families. This food drive was a group effort by Farm Share, the Alachua County Christian Pastors Association, and The Long Foundation.

¡SALVEN A LOS ABUELOS!

» **BY HELEN MOREJÓN**

Los pulmones sabios
Lágrimas derrochan,
Arrodillados ante la muerte
Misericordia imploran,
A los médicos jueces
Que a la vejez no perdonan,
Priorizando al respiro joven
Mientras los ancianos se ahogan.
Como si las canas familia no tuvieran,
Como si a la vida no quisieran.

¡Salven a los abuelos!

Muriendo en camillas de hospitales,
Sus carnes cremadas por extraños,
Creencias y derechos olvidados,
Mientras las viudas ajenas a sus pérdidas,
Aun rezan en sus cuarentenas,
Por la recuperación de sus almas gemelas.

¡Salven a los abuelos!

Save the Grandparents!
The wise lungs
Tears squander,
Kneeling before death
They implore mercy,
To the medical judges
Who without compassion,
Prioritize the young breath
While the old men drown.
As if gray hair did not have a family,
As if their lives did not matter.
Save the grandparents!

Dying on hospital stretchers,
Their flesh cremated by strangers,
Beliefs and rights are forgotten.
While the widows, oblivious to their losses,
Still, pray in their quarantine loneliness,
For the recovery of their soul mates.

Save the grandparents!

Helen Morejón is a pre-health student at the University of Florida doing a Bachelor's in Applied Physiology and Kinesiology. Born in Havana, Cuba, Helen came to the United States at the age of thirteen with her mother, to be reunited with her father after ten years of being apart. She has competed in the U.S. Chess's Nationals and has volunteered her time for organizations such as Feeding South Florida, Special Olympics, UF Health Shands Hospital, Kinetix Physical Therapy Clinic, and many others. She has also worked as a research assistant for Renne Lab. Her passions are writing poems and photography.

COPING

» BY SANDY LEVEEN

When I was young, I spent my summers with my grandmother in Elm Creek, Nebraska, not wearing shoes or seeing friends or other family members from the time school was out in the spring until it resumed in the fall. I got fat, became more and more isolated, losing touch with playmates, and not coming out of my "shell" for the rest of my life. I am not a stranger to solitude, isolation, and loneliness.

Sheltering in place is not new to me.

As an adult, I have tried hard to put this all behind me. I have pushed myself into social interaction through exercise and activities I enjoy, such as gardening, biking, and tennis.

Now along comes COVID. My husband and I, being of a certain age, are following the CDC guidelines to the letter, wearing facemasks and social distancing when we go out, but mostly sheltering in place. We have eaten lots of home cooked meals and I have watched a lot of Turner Classic movies and reread many classics from my own bookshelves or from the library via my Overdrive app.

It is my garden that has made all the difference to my state of mind. Because of the wild creatures that visit my garden daily, I feel connected to the outside world.

I have hope.

The little hummingbird that visits my firecracker plant and my fire bush plant "talks" to me every morning, as he hovers near where I sit on my screened porch. The Zebra Long Wing and Gulf Fritillary butterflies are in abundance, laying their eggs on my Passion Flower vine, one even coming too close to an Anole and ending up as lunch. Life and death in the garden. I have only to look to the sky as I hear the "Phee-Phew" of the Mississippi Kite that migrates through our area to know that life goes on. I feel very lucky to have these symbols of normalcy in this unsettling time. I find the uprooted plants and the spilled watering cans that I see during my morning stroll in the garden reassuring. Day and night, life goes on.

Sandy LeVeen is a retired elementary school teacher currently living in Gainesville Florida. Her interests include gardening (she is a Master Gardener in Alachua County), painting, and writing. As an essayist, her pieces have appeared in many local publications. She has read her work on two NPR affiliate stations, one in her native Nebraska and one in Florida. Humor is an integral part of her writing style and her artwork. She recently had a photo titled "Shut" in a juried exhibition at the Harn Museum of Art in Gainesville.

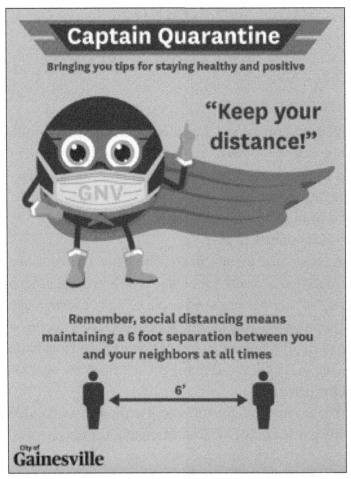

(PHOTO BY DUSTIN WALSH)

"Captain Quarantine was created in order to promote fun and positivity during the pandemic by delivering positive messages, reminders and helpful tips. . . during the stay-at-home order."

– Dustin Walsh, marketing and communications specialist for the City of Gainesville.

MY PANDEMIC EXPERIENCE

» BY PATTIE MACURDY

Conveniently, the coronavirus stay-at-home requirement coincided with a time when I would have stayed home anyway due to my worsening arthritic, walking disability. I was ninety, but determined to socialize. Once a week, with much help from my son, I got seated in my power chair on my back porch to receive guests for a two-hour period. We took all the precautions. Chairs were positioned six feet apart, and we wore masks. Seating for five was about the limit and made for good conversation.

Most of my guests were members of the Writers Alliance of Gainesville (WAG) or Life History writers, so the conversations were lively and entertaining. Topics included childhood, whether we modeled our parents' behavior, laughably meager royalties for books published, racism, Loquat trees, dream interpretation, and bird calls.

Spring weather was perfect for these outdoor get-togethers, which were said to be healthier than gathering inside where dangerously contagious viruses linger longer in the air. My back porch was perfect. With a wooded lot beside me and an open field behind me, birds were plentiful. Wrens, chickadees, cardinals, blue jays, and owls serenaded us as though they were in choir practice.

The sessions ended when my self-allotted two-hour time was up and I telephoned my son to appear. Using a special borrowed ramp, he could retrieve me and my power chair from the porch. Nobody wanted to stop talking, so we would plan it again for the following week.

I think I coped well under these difficult stay-at-home circumstances. We all wished for a longer spring season. Up through May, we enjoyed lovely seventy-five to eighty-degree, breezy afternoons, but soon my porch was too hot and the mosquitoes moved in.

A new method of meeting while socially distancing was needed to get us through the hot summer. Learning Zoom was fun, and it works quite well for some meetings, but it is not the same as seeing friends in person. A COVID-19 vaccine, or therapeutic drug, can't come soon enough. We hope for the scientists to bring us a Christmas gift of safely socializing the old-fashioned way with shared loving hugs and the needed human touch. We miss each other.

After growing up as a farm girl in rural Tennessee, Pattie Macurdy traveled the world as wife of a U.S. Air Force fighter pilot. Now ninety-one, she lives and writes near the University of Florida in Gainesville. Pattie's published book, *Sunsets and Blizzards,* is a collection of true stories about her colorful life. Some stories can also be found on her blog, pattieremembers.wordpress.com. Expect humor and sadness. The stories are authentic.

MY LIFE IN THE TIME OF CORONAVIRUS

» BY RONNIE LOVLER

It's not exactly akin to *The Year of Living Dangerously*, but there is something about the current situation that brings that movie to mind. Maybe it's simply the title that makes me think of my weeks of living dangerously each time I go to the supermarket or pharmacy and expose myself to other people. Or the moments when I really lived dangerously and invited a friend to sit on my back porch to share a bottle of wine while we sat a safe six feet apart.

I, of course, am not living dangerously, not when I compare my relative seclusion and seductive self-isolation to the brave and selfless actions of health care workers, first responders, and essential service personnel. However, just like everyone else, my life is very different from what I had envisioned for myself before COVID-19.

For starters, there were my travel plans, now squelched, of course. The journey to Portugal and Spain that was to have occurred in May is not happening. The trip to Baltimore to visit my son in late March and see the cherry blossoms in Washington, DC—cancelled. An editor's conference in Salt Lake City—gone with the wind. During one of my endless days at home, I came across the travel section of *The New York Times* from Sunday, Jan. 12 that highlighted fifty-two places to go in 2020. Hmm, I've got a lot of catching up to do. So far, my "travel" list is topped by almost daily visits to two city parks. Call it waddling for wellness, keeping my Fitbit and me happy as I get in my 10,000 steps. The walks bookend my day—coffee and two miles in the morning, wine and two miles in the evening.

I seek to hold onto the good in a not very good situation. I know I am among the lucky ones. I struggle to find contentment, if not unbridled happiness. The presence of two little girls who live in my neighborhood and ride their bikes past my window every day cheers me up.

I have been in semi-lockdown since March 23, when Alachua County issued its Emergency Order 2020-09, aptly titled, "It is Time to Shelter in Place—Stay at Home." My social and work life now revolve around Zoom, my new best friend, because it allows me to stay socially connected, even as I remain socially distant.

I now conduct my classes on public speaking and online writing via Zoom. I attend political events and board meetings on Zoom. My writer's group meets on Zoom. I attend lectures from international journalists and academics on Zoom. And for fun, I am a regular at a weekly Zoom dance party with people from Michigan.

I meet up with a friend three or four times a week to watch Jeopardy together, courtesy of Zoom. I go to Zoom happy hours and on occasion attend Shabbat services on Zoom from my local reform synagogue.

I attended two family Passover Seders on Zoom with matzo ball soup and other Passover staples at our respective locations. Zoom twice facilitated two wonderful hours of family time.

I am reeling off this list, because Zoom helps keeps me sane. I don't feel like I am in solitary confinement, in great part thanks to Zoom. The gallery view on Zoom is like the clip from the movie *Love Actually*. I love seeing everyone's face and hearing their voices. I relish being alone together.

Zoom isn't everything, and I do have other diversions. My friends and family share funny videos that are COVID related. One I particularly like is a montage of video clips, most likely from Spain, that include scenes of people playing ping pong from window to window in an apartment building.

There are truly extraordinary and moving videos shared, like the French National Orchestra playing Ravel's Bolero with each musician at home. Other offerings have included the Metropolitan Opera's free live streaming of nightly operas. My favorite late night talk show hosts haven't skipped a beat and are broadcasting from home.

What else do I do to pass the time? I maintain social connectivity outside of Zoom with one or two lengthy phone calls each day with a friend or family member, often with people with whom I had lapsed in terms of staying in touch.

I have signed up for French and German classes on Duolingo, a language-learning app. Sometimes I wonder why I bother, when travel to countries where French or German is spoken is definitely not in my immediate future. But hope beats eternal.

I also read and watch movies. I have about thirty books lined up to read both online and in hardcover editions. I have subscriptions to Amazon and Netflix and get HBO and Starz with my cable subscription, which I had been about to cancel until the pandemic kept me home. I also just rediscovered Turner Classic Movies.

There are, of course, moments of sadness and stress, as we watch the death toll spiral and collectively shake our heads at the lack of leadership exhibited by our perplexing president. I am frustrated at being hailed as a "superhero" just for staying at home. I wanted to do something to help. I went to a local website looking for volunteers but was hit with the news that I was too old and should stay home. I rebelled in a fashion by walking over to my local blood bank where I left behind a pint of my blood. So at least I am not too old and at too much at risk for that!

So that's my coronavirus story. Here I am now going to borrow from the 1948 film and later television series *The Naked City*, which said "There are eight million stories in the naked city. This has been one of them." In our times, there are tens, if not hundreds of millions of coronavirus stories to tell; mine is one of them.

PASSING THROUGH THE PANDEMIC PORTAL

» BY JOE COURTER

Most of us were seeing the reports out of China, and then Italy, in early 2020. We saw they were taking measures to deal with the virus, but it seemed so far away. That all changed in early March. New York City reported its first case March 1ˢᵗ and in a week was taking strong measures. With close friends in New York, the reality of what we were facing became tangible, along with the knowledge that their reality would soon be ours.

The reality began to hit for me here in Gainesville the weekend of March 13ᵗʰ-15ᵗʰ. I went to a music show at the Civic Media Center that Friday night, the last show the CMC has had up to now. No one was masked yet, but I knew this was not wise in light of what we were hearing from elsewhere. I knew older people were at higher risk, and being decades older than anyone at the show, it was in my head. On Saturday, I spent the evening with a good friend downtown at The Top, sitting at the bar, no masks in sight. We talked a lot about what was coming. She is a physician's assistant, and we both knew these carefree days were over. And then on Sunday, I took my last excursion with other people, a trip on the drawn-down Ocklawaha River to see the springs that would disappear when Rodman dam again overflows the river. It was a last pre-COVID fling.

I have not eaten in a restaurant since. No more going out to live music shows, a passion of mine. No more handshakes and, more importantly, hugs... I live alone, and hugs from people are important to me. A good friend works in a store, and in late April, after my purchase, we had a solid hug across the counter, quite spontaneously. I had a tear in my eye as I left. I am pretty well-grounded, and this made me aware of how hard this period would be for others.

The biggest change I witnessed was the functioning of the Civic Media Center, a place I am heavily involved in as a co-founder, board member, and volunteer. Pre-pandemic, it was a hotbed of activity with music shows, meetings, art shows, poetry jams. Boom! With the exception of the Free Grocery Store, we shut down. This started as a once-a-week effort where people came to get free vegetables, breads and pastries, and other donated items.

The volunteers running this got busy and reorganized for COVID. Operating with full safety procedures, volunteers made it a distribution hub for free food, bringing food weekly to the doorsteps of over 300 people in need. The CMC was there, able to change with the times, and the volunteers were eager to step up and grateful to have meaningful work to do in the crisis. It is a testament to active community organizing, not only having the physical resource, but attracting and nurturing people in civic responsibility and good works.

I also am the publisher of the *Gainesville Iguana*, a semi-monthly newsletter and calendar of events. We kept up publishing, but without the calendar of events because events in our vibrant town ground to a halt. But we have been able to profile mutual aid, housing struggles, as well as reports on the virus itself. All the dynamic activities, marches and protests, as well as electoral politics, so prominent in the last nine months, actually increased a sense of purpose to those efforts. Distribution took a hit, with many locations closed, but we have kept going. There's certainly no shortage of material to report on in these times.

So how is my life different? With more time at home, I'm fixing things up around here. Being almost 70 and finally about to start getting Social Security, I damn sure do not want to cut my life short by being careless, so I have very much limited my social contacts and happily wear a mask if I am around people. Since I'm not going out to music shows, I am drinking less beer and eating better at home rather than catching fast food somewhere. I am on my bike more, I am lucky to have a nice eastern view from the house for sunrises, and I will often travel into town to view sunsets from Paynes Prairie or the downtown parking garage. Those daily events are an excellent time of reflection, coming with their own time limit, then moving on to other things. And I am taking more time to read actual books, not just off my computer screen.

I am the main human contact for my 85-year-old mother-in-law, who is isolating and probably at high risk should she catch the virus. This has made me more careful and conscious. I had one notable slip up, on election night November 3rd, when I went to a friend's house for a watch party. People were limited and it was outside on a patio with a big screen TV. Those early returns did not look good, and somehow we six people ended up inside, in the living room, unmasked. I had a big wtf moment, and left shortly after, chalking it up to alcohol and distraction by the less than stellar results. Eight days later, I got a text from the host. She and her partner had tested positive. I made calls and got booked into Shands to get a nasal swab test. It came back negative, but it was a real perspective enhancer.

In April, Arundhati Roy wrote, "Pandemics are a portal," and when we come out the other side, things are different. How will this wind down? When can we enjoy the old normal? Crowded music shows? Warm hugs with friends? Going out to eat and drink with carefree feelings? Will it take years to feel that free again? For many, there may be no going back as employers and colleges find they can save a buck with remote operations. We are in a transition, passing through the pandemic portal. We need to be sensible, patient, and embrace the knowledge gained through science. And with that, I hope that wisdom and empathy can come to the forefront and get us beyond the rancorous divide the last half decade has given us.

Joe Courter grew up in New Jersey and graduated college in Michigan with a Psychology/Sociology major. After two years in Colorado, he moved to Gainesville in 1975. He has been self-employed, doing various work, mostly house painting. He co-founded the Gainesville *Iguana Newsmonthly* in 1986. In 1993, he was a co-founder of the Civic Media Center. He is still involved in the latter two endeavors as publisher and board member, respectively. He loves music, biking, reading, and the outdoors.

TO WHOM IT MAY CONCERN

» BY CONNIE DOBY

To whom it may concern,

I'm a native of Florida, lived here in Gainesville all my 49 years, and living here during this time is truly historic. I was actually having that conversation with my 13-year-old a couple of weeks ago, saying this will probably one day be in history books and one day the kids that were not born during this time will read about what you lived through. Living with this new normal way of life has been a challenge but I know this too will pass, and right now we're all safer at home. Every day during the week I have a routine of getting up, cleaning and sanitizing the most touched surfaces and objects in the house. Then I have breakfast and make sure I get my son up and moving to do his 8th grade schoolwork online, realizing that there will most likely be no 8th grade field trips, 8th grade social or end-of-the-year recognition ceremony for him as we had for his previous three siblings before him. But then I think again and say, he's safe and that's more important, and we will just have to do something for him a little different is all, after I've had my fill of inside activities, and Netflix, etc....

I do go outside for my daily dose of sunshine and to enjoy what I can of the daylight. This makes you really miss the simple things like just getting up to get ready for work and other adult social interactions, going out to eat lunch or dinner, or just simple trips to the grocery store without having to have masks and/or gloves, and parties with your family. It may be a while still before we can have some sense of normalcy, but until then we will stay safer at home.

Connie Doby is a native Gainesvillian and Floridian who works as a secretary at the University of Florida. All of her immediate family still lives here as well, including her parents, four kids, and four grandchildren. They are all Gator fans, of course, and her husband, youngest son, oldest son, and oldest grandson have been involved with City Recreation Youth Sports for well over nine or ten years, as volunteers in one form or the other. It's a way of giving back to the community that they love.

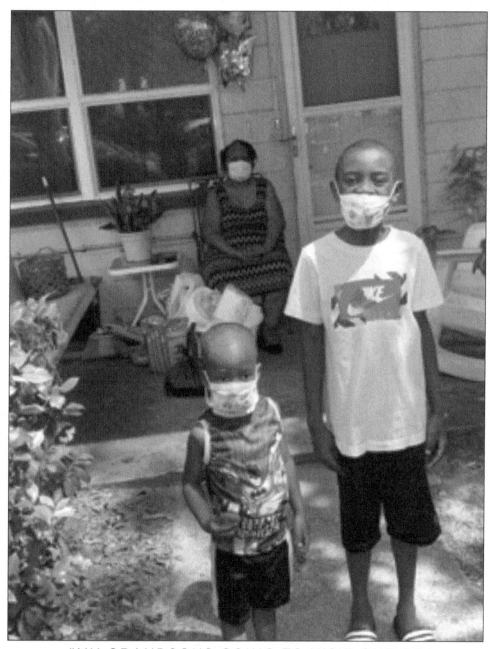

"MY GRANDSONS GOING TO VISIT ONE OF THEIR GREAT-GRANDMOTHERS FOR HER BIRTHDAY" (PHOTO BY CONNIE DOBY)

CHAPTER 4

A STEEP LEARNING CURVE: BALANCING EDUCATION AND A PANDEMIC

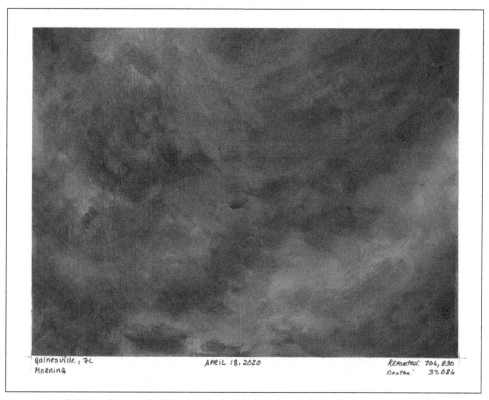

gainesville, FL
Morning

APRIL 18, 2020

REported: 706,830
Deaths: 37,086

APRIL 18, 2020 (GWENDOLYN CHRZANOWSKI)

STUCK AND CONFUSED

» BY BLAIR DE LAS ALAS

Everything in front of me looks like a blur. Maybe because everyone is moving too fast? I sit here and think, but maybe thinking is why I am slower than them. They look proud, vibrant, and prepared—all opposite of me, or maybe I am just a bit too worried? The beginning of 2020, I did not stand strong to it; I started weak, paranoid, and tired, thinking that the year would give me another chance to redeem myself.

"Have you heard the news? A new virus was discovered a few days ago."

"Maybe it isn't too bad."

A few months have passed since I heard about the news and gossip. So far, so good. I'm almost finished coloring this page, a small assignment given to me each week by my previous English teacher, to assess a definition of a chosen word to enhance my vocabulary. I mind my own business until I hear her requesting me and a few boys to arrange the chairs in the multi-purpose room. After completing the task, I return to the class, hearing her announce something important.

"There is a possibility that you may not be in class for a few weeks or so, due to the new virus reaching the county, so a quarantine may happen."

An initial breath of relief and giddy excitement floods the classroom. I, too, feel joy, thinking that I can finally take a little break to recollect myself for a few weeks, only to later realize how much of a mistake it was to think that way. I am not the type of person to stay at home and only home, because where I live, this is not my home. It is a place filled with cold tension due to living with certain people I do not… appreciate, to say the least. I normally visit my peers to do my work and have fun. When I realize quarantine keeps me from that, I start to feel a little sour. Every day I feel stuck, and every moment I wake up, I feel heavier. I start to regret hoping to feel good about the quarantine break. I start to regret hoping, overall.

Every moment I feel helpless, as if my body does not belong. I start rapidly gaining weight from staying still for months, I want to move, but I am locked in, so I keep standing still. My heart begins beating faster, but I'm not running, no—my body has changed. I am no longer healthy. My mind becomes tainted and I start to go blind. Blinded with pent up anger and sadness. That's when things get worse for me. I get easily agitated from a small mishap, and I isolate myself from everyone else.

Sadness covers me like a warm blanket, giving me a false sense of security. Even though I had this problem earlier, before the pandemic, it exacerbated afterwards. The change in lifestyle may have been the cause.

I begin to wonder, "Could I have prepared for this?"

Surely not. I don't think anyone was prepared for this, at all. From everyone's appearance around me, they begin to slow down to my pace as well, their features getting clearer, but their faces look… sad, to say the least. And then I know, it isn't just me who is affected by this situation. They may not be in the same situation, but their emotions have similarities, primarily the feeling of being stuck and confused.

Things started clearing up a little, but not too much. I still had to get used to a lot of things. After a while of being stuck, I started moving a little bit more, hoping I would change a little as well. Bit by bit, I try to calm myself down, recollect my day, and think about things that happened. Almost a year has passed since this whole mess happened, so I might as well change this before I get stuck in the next one.

I remind myself that I can be strong and independent when I am willing enough to be. I can't guarantee that it will work the whole time, but I am slowly getting back on my game, and I am growing more confident that I can fix most of what was ripped apart from me.

Blair De Las Alas, a seventeen-year-old student, aspires to work in a medical field. In first grade, she discovered a simplistic example of biology. After moving to the United States, she started strong and passionate, taking careful measures of her work to send the right message. This resulted in teachers' proud attention, giving her an easy advantage. Nowadays, she struggles to find that same spark. Even though she doesn't burn as bright, the dim spark is enough to help her stand up and find herself, piece by piece, hoping that one day she can be that same person her mentors were proud of.

COVID WORRIES

» **BY JOSEPH GARCISO**

COVID has affected my life, but not as much as others, due to the fact that I am more like a hermit that does not go out often. It still has negatively affected me, of course. When school was starting again, I wanted to do Brick and Mortar. My reasoning was because I knew if I did online, I would easily get distracted at home. Unsurprisingly, this is what is happening, and it is a terrible thing. I really do not want to fail. It is something that I am scared of, not only because of failing, but also how my parents would react.

While I do enjoy a free excuse to stay home, it has affected my grades in a way that is not favorable. It has been hard for me when it comes to schoolwork. I get distracted by something, and it takes away my attention. It also does not help that I forget to do my homework.

There are also my two grandmas that live with us. So my family wants to be really careful, as it would be terrible if our grandma got infected when she is still recovering from the weeks spent in the hospital.

That really is all that I can think of, other than seeing my parents more often. That is not important enough to talk about, though. So all in all, it was great over summer for someone that just sits in their own home, but it became a negative thing when school started again.

Joseph Garciso is in twelfth grade at Gainesville High School.

THE WAYS COVID HAS AFFECTED MY LIFE

» **BY MAKAYLA MAYHEW**

There are tons of ways COVID has affected my life. One way is not being able to hang out with my friends as much. Another way is always having to wear a mask. The last way it has affected my life is how school works.

The first way COVID has affected my life is me not being able to hang out with my friends as much as I used to. Normally, I would spend almost every weekend at the river, or the springs, or somewhere with my friends, just to live in the moment. We can't do that every weekend. But we still do it from time to time in smaller numbers of people, and we wear masks when we are not in the water. Sometimes, if the river looks like there are too many people there, we'll just go hang out at a park or someplace else that's open enough for us to be safe, and we still wear a mask.

Another way that COVID has affected my life is having to wear a mask. I never used to wear a mask, like most people did not. When COVID first started up around last March, I didn't really think it was a big deal and I never took it seriously, until I saw that it was real and I actually saw how big the pandemic is, and that was when I started taking it seriously and started wearing my masks and social distancing.

Lastly, COVID has affected my life by how me and tons of other people go to school. This year is the first year my teachers have ever had to do Zoom classes. I do not really like Zoom because I don't feel like I'm learning as much as I would in the classroom, but I only have to do it for about two weeks. I also feel like sometimes Zoom is good because I have been able to catch up on a lot of stuff I had been behind on.

Those are the ways that COVID has affected my life. The good and the bad.

Makayla Mayhew is a senior at Gainesville High School.

MY SENIOR YEAR LOST TO COVID

» BY ELLIE JOHNSON

COVID has affected my school activities and changed the way I interact with people in general. COVID has changed the way I spend my off time. Not only has it changed interactions with others, but how we clean items we buy at the grocery store or at a roadside market before bringing them into the house. COVID-19 ruined my senior year of high school. This is why I really don't care for the COVID virus.

Due to COVID-19, we are only allowed to have a small number of people attending events, and everyone has to wear a mask. Most places check our temperature as part of the screening process. At school and in the community, we have to maintain a six-foot distance, wear a mask, and wash our hands if we touch any surface in public. It's also hard on the teachers because they have to clean everything in between classes. Which brings up a good question, who's cleaning the toilets between every use?

COVID has changed my off-time. Since COVID-19, my mother has been very strict on me wearing a mask and keeping my hands clean. She doesn't allow me to roam the mall or go to movie theaters, like normal teenagers used to do. Even at the beach and lake, which are open areas, she still will not let me go, due to possible overcrowding, or someone there may be a carrier of COVID. She knows me well enough to know I probably would not have on my mask, and the wind could possibly blow the particles up my nose or in my mouth, thus exposing me to the coronavirus.

The one thing that I am allowed to do is on Sunday. I get to spend my day at the paintball field, where I am expected to wear a mask under my full paintball headgear and not touch other players. These rules are strictly enforced by the team captains. Trust me, the captains of my team know my mom very well, to the point where they make me behave.

Back to the topic above. I haven't truly expressed my feelings. If we are as scared as some of us claim to be, why don't we have a "No touch" rule? People who test positive for COVID can STILL go out to stores to buy food. Who is to say they washed their hands? How do we know they didn't cough into their hands, then touch fruit?

I have a fear of going to my own grocery store and bringing stuff back to my grandparents' house without stopping by my house first to scrub everything! It isn't even COVID that I'm worried about. Think about how many people have touched that apple before you, or that loaf of bread. How many people don't wash their hands after leaving the bathroom, then come into a store and touch fruit, milk cartons, or meat packages? I always wipe down stuff I buy from stores, whether it be food, toys, or clothes. I make sure to clean everything. COVID is just making me wipe things twice or more. The fear of bringing something besides groceries home scares me. I do my best to kill germs and the bugs hiding in the items.

In conclusion, COVID has taken almost everything, even things I haven't addressed. I don't get a Prom, every girl's dream. I don't get to go to Gradbash, something every high school kid talks about for years after graduation. At this point, I don't think my school will even be having a graduation ceremony like the years before me. One of the biggest things I looked forward to was walking across the stage with my friends and family cheering me on.

I hate COVID. It has taken EVERYTHING from me. I have anxiety when I go to the store, in fear that I might bring something home. I don't get to go buy a dress with my friends. I don't get to dance the night away. I don't get to experience being a Senior, and it truly hurts. So there it is, laid out on the line for everyone to know how I really feel. COVID sucks. COVID has taken an important part of my life that I won't be able to get back. So thank you, COVID. I've lost almost my entire senior experience to you.

Ellie Johnson is a senior at Gainesville High School.

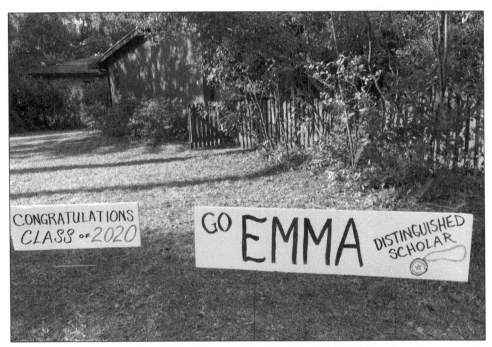

(PHOTO BY PHOEBE PAPADI)

"I made these signs to honor a friend's granddaughter who lives just down the street. She is graduating from high school this year, and will not have the usual ceremony because of COVID."

– Phoebe Papadi

THE CORONAVIRUS'S EFFECT ON THE STUDENT POPULATION AT THE UNIVERSITY OF FLORIDA

» **BY JANE PEREZ**

Once, Turlington Plaza was the central hub of UF's social scene as it sat between Marston Library and Turlington Hall, while also serving as the intersection of the east and west sides of campus. The vast number of tables and busy foot traffic gave an opportunity for student interactions as Greek life promoted their houses, political parties campaigned, and clubs fundraised for their cause. Previously, students would walk with earphones, specifically to avoid the hub and bub, and now not a single student is to be found as classes became canceled and the libraries closed.

TURLINGTON PLAZA, UNIVERSITY OF FLORIDA (PHOTO BY JANE PEREZ)

The only constant presence now is the chiming of Century Tower and the forgotten bicycles chained to the stands. Students are left without a space to study at Marston Library—a necessity for students who have disruptive homes or learning disabilities that cause them to be easily distracted. Students that prioritize being well-rounded, with good grades and extracurricular activities, are only left with a subpar teaching method in Zoom, rather than walking to their classroom at Turlington Hall and taking part in social functions at the plaza. What was once a place of learning and character growth has become a bare venue while students are left to work with only their computers and possibly a desk, if they have one at all.

Ben Hill Griffin Stadium, otherwise called "The Swamp," has held over 90,000 screaming football fans during the peak season. At first glance, this stadium looks as desolate as the rest of campus; instead, it is swarming with students exercising and families touring. Dozens—if not a hundred—people spread out through the stadium. They climb the stairs, stretch on the field, and run laps along the interior. Some families perform their own tours as UF's facilitated guides were canceled. Families come wearing masks, with future students excited by the possibility of starting a new chapter in their life and scared that their college experience will be dashed by the coronavirus. Parents are worried about the amount of people in what feels like such close proximity after the emptiness of the rest of UF's campus. But it can also make one wonder about what an extended coronavirus will mean for the future: will football season be canceled in the fall because of COVID-19? While a seemingly trivial question, it will undoubtedly have effects on the student body and school as a source of moral and financial gain. How will schools continue if they do not make money from sports or "gator gear" or housing? This brings up an alarming question for schools nationwide as we consider every possible way coronavirus will alter this country and the world.

The Plaza of the Americas is known for its Krishna lunch, comfortable hammocks, and crowded walkways. On bright and sunny days, students lounge on the green grass to socialize, study, or both. Nicely wedged between two libraries, two class halls, and the financial aid office, there was no lack of people walking through this plaza, and its shady trees and soft grass made it a prime place to spend in-between classes. Now this beautiful day is left with few admirers: me, a passerby, and this one couple in a hammock. Before, blocking a walkway would be unthinkable, but now this hammock is not a deterrent for anyone. Instead, only one student walks through the plaza: with only her mask and backpack, she is determined to stay safe and focused on the path ahead of her. She does not look at anyone as she keeps her eyes on the ground and does not notice me until I approach her. She did not mind me taking her picture but was quick to move along afterwards. It shows that this is not a time for friendly conversation or meeting new people, but a time of cautiousness where you only leave your home out of necessity. I wanted to ask her why she did decide to leave her house at all, but she was already gone. Did she have work? Did she need fresh air to study? Did she leave her dorm to get groceries? Does it even matter?

Jane T. Perez is a student at the University of Florida. Born to a Cuban immigrant father and American mother, Jane has an interest in US and Latin American politics. As a history and political science major, she took the course Headlines to Histories, a seminar focused on how people perceive famous events and their actuality. In the middle of the semester, COVID-19 struck. Her professor, Dr. Louise Newman, asked her students to reflect on COVID, the actuality, impact, and future perception of this pandemic. Since the beginning of the pandemic, Jane has been inspired to write and work on her undergraduate thesis on homophobia in the Caribbean. She hopes to pursue a master's in Latin American studies and have a career in foreign policy.

FINDING POSITIVES IN THE COVID EXPERIENCE

» **BY CAMRYN MUELLER**

COVID-19 hit us all hard, yet differently. As a student, it was a difficult challenge to overcome. One minute having classes on campus and then changing to online was a bit of a challenge, but it wasn't impossible. It was a hard adjustment, but at the end of the day, it wasn't the worst thing. I never took online classes for a reason, and that is because I am a hands-on learner. I enjoy the environment of campus, meeting new people and learning in a classroom. Transitioning to online classes was hard at the beginning, but going through this transition was the least of my worries.

My job as a receptionist was something I was scared to lose with COVID-19 just starting. I was able to stay employed by working remotely. Nannying stayed the same for me; I worked with my one family during the quarantine. Working remotely and going to school online was really challenging, but I am blessed. I looked at this experience differently. This was only going to make me stronger and become a better student and employee. I will admit, it hasn't been easy, but I am thankful for the experience. As a student, I am always caught in a moment where I think things are "too hard," but it turns out, the more I grow, the better I become. Over this time, it has allowed me to reflect on myself and the person I want to become. If something difficult comes my way, I will overcome it. I will adjust to it. I will become stronger through it. Although the situation isn't an ideal way to learn these things, I am grateful for the experiences I have learned through it.

The unknown is the scariest part about this whole situation. My grandmother has many medical problems. She is a high-risk person to get the virus. She is vulnerable to getting sick quickly. It is scary to know she cannot go to her regular appointments due to the virus. Her appointments were constantly changing, since places were closing and fewer people could be seen by doctors. Although she has many medical issues, this didn't stop them from canceling her appointments to keep her safe, but it also kept her from getting the help she needed. Watching all this happen was heartbreaking; I just wanted her to get the help she could. I did not understand why it was vital for her to not go to the necessary appointments. I was fearful for her. She needed specific procedures that she just couldn't get at the time. They were not scheduling unnecessary surgeries. I thought she needed these surgeries, but the doctors did not think they were necessary at the time.

This gave me the time to talk to her more. I was so busy with my life; I would forget to call and check up on her. Once COVID-19 started, it allowed me to have more time to talk to my loved ones and check on them. My life was always so busy, and I never took a minute to reach out to them. I reflected on myself during this time. This reflection time allowed me to understand the importance of taking a moment out of my "busy" life and talking to them.

Overall, this time has been an eye-opener for me. I have become stronger through this. I now know anything is possible if you don't give up. Transitioning from in-class to online was a challenge, but it is do-able. I am still able to meet new people through virtual meetings for class, and I am able to be outgoing. I am growing through this period in my life, figuring out how to cope with everything that has happened. Adjusting to something new is a battle you face within yourself. It is possible to overcome the adjustment if you just find good in what you think is terrible.

I have turned this situation into something positive. I have learned to take more time out of my busy day to talk to my family. Spend time with your loved ones. My family and I now play games every night. We talk so much more than we used to. I was too busy to even think I had time to play a game. This time has taught me so much. I am thankful for the knowledge I have now and the way I view my time. Call the family you don't get to see often and check on them. Take the time to reflect on what is important to you. This has been an experience I will hold on to forever.

Camryn Mueller grew up in a small town, Newberry, Florida, where everyone knows everyone. She went to school with the same group of people her whole life. She played volleyball throughout high school and made a lot of friendships that she cherishes. Now a full-time student at Santa Fe College, she works as a receptionist and a nanny. She also has a photography business that she does on weekends. She enjoys staying busy and meeting new people.

CORONAVIRUS EXPERIENCE

» BY PALACE NIEKERK

When I first heard about COVID-19 in March, I was very anxious about it. The media was telling us that it was basically the end of the world. So many rumors were made up about where the virus came from, what it did to people, and how we were going to "get rid of it." All anyone could do was worry.

I was working at a fast-food restaurant when the pandemic broke out. Not one single precaution was taken. When the dining room was supposed to be closed, it was open. When the employees were supposed to be wearing masks and gloves, they weren't. It was a hot mess. I, being a type 2 diabetic, told my boss I had to cut down on my hours due to being at high risk. He denied me that request. He told me he needed me to work more hours. It almost felt as if he didn't believe I was a diabetic. I came to my parents with my dilemma. They told me I had to quit my job since my health comes first, and they were failing to be safe at work.

Once I quit my job, I became very depressed. My girlfriend and I broke up. I had no reliable source of income, all my friends were moving home, and my online classes were getting the best of me. I thought I was losing everything, which caused me to lose myself. I started to become very isolated and unmotivated, which then affected my sleep and my overall daily routine.

I ended up having to voluntarily Baker Act myself because I started getting concerned for my safety. All I could think about when sitting in the hospital was all the germs being passed around. Masks were not mandatory or handed out, which left me with even more anxiety. On top of not feeling safe from COVID, I was not being treated for my diabetes. They failed to take my blood sugar, failed to give me my blood sugar stabilizing medications, and failed to feed me a healthy diet. When my blood sugar is unstable, my moods and attitudes become unstable. After twenty-seven hours, I ended up signing myself out. I felt like I was getting crazier and crazier by the minute.

My parents suggested I come home for a while until I could find a job back in Gainesville. I was home for three weeks when I landed a job as a driver at Papa John's Pizza. At my interview, I asked how they were taking safety precautions, and they told me everything I wanted to hear. And they were. Only a certain number of people are allowed in the store, every guest and team member has to wear a mask, and we are offering contactless delivery. I have been working there for a couple months now and am making steady money. They are flexible with their hours and have great respect for their employees. I couldn't be happier working for this company.

Although COVID got the best of me at the beginning, I was able to bounce back from it and set a different routine, one that would make me feel safer and happier.

Always remember to wash your hands and wear a mask.

Palace Niekerk is a student at Santa Fe College

SCHOOL DAZE: GETTING AN EDUCATION IN COVID TIMES

» **BY BONNIE OGLE**

Taylor Luttrell, a senior at the University of Florida, confirms what we all suspected: "The spring semester of school was just plain hard! Staying home and doing classes online was definitely not the convenience I'd thought it might be. Being able to interact with fellow students, and particularly with professors, was sorely missed. Three-hour block classes on Zoom were difficult, and time management was a huge problem."

In the beginning, when in-person classes were shut down, Taylor returned to her parents' home in North Carolina. By the end of the semester, doing school online became easier, and group chats with fellow students helped combat isolation. The fall semester was easier, returning to campus for live classes. Graduates at all schools found year-end recognition and celebrations curtailed or modified. The traditional "Walk" became a "pose" in the living room with cap and gown as a student's name was called out.

Using a virtual platform, organization was hard for professors, as well. Having to develop classes online was a challenge. Many were stressed, not having the required technical know-how. One friend, a physics professor, had recorded lectures, which saved time and reinvention of the wheel. Another, a math professor, was accustomed to precision, and having to "jump right in" with no technical training was especially taxing.

My high school neighbor, on the P. K. Yonge varsity football team, went back to full-time classes in the fall, after all online classes in the spring. He said sports were the same but with extra precautions.

And we've all seen the changes in Gator sports. Even season ticket holders watched football games from home, as seating at Ben Hill Griffin Stadium was severely limited at 17,000, about twenty percent of its 88,548 capacity. There was no tailgating on campus or spirit teams or cheerleaders on the sidelines. Gator Walk, where fans get up close to players, Gator Walk Village, and Gators Fan Fest did not happen during the 2020 season.

However, like other college and NFL teams, fans had the opportunity to be there—well, for their faces to be there. For $99 a fan could purchase a 2.75-foot-tall cutout of themselves which was fastened to a seat for all home games. While recorded fan noise was played by some schools, Taylor attested that all games this year were "calmer, quieter." Even the Cotton Bowl in Texas, which she and a friend drove to, was quieter. Fans were seated in "pods," with those who had purchased tickets together, seated together.

Generally, the student perspective on life during the pandemic is the same as that of the general population, and well voiced by Lake Superior University. Since 1976, wordsmiths at the school have produced a yearly list of words that should be banned from the English Language. This year "COVID-19" is number one on the list. Some banned phrases include "We're all in this together," "An abundance of caution," and "In these uncertain times." All in all, the COVID experience for students and everyone else has been unprecedented. Oops, pardon me. The word unprecedented was also banned.

CHAPTER 5
PANDEMIC POLITICS

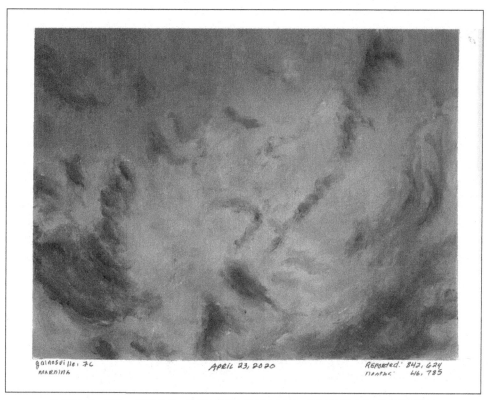

gainesville, FC
MARDING

APRIL 23, 2020

REPORTED: 842, 624
Deaths: 46, 785

APRIL 23, 2020 (GWENDOLYN CHRZANOWSKI)

CONTEMPORARY COMMENTARY

» **BY ERIC DIAMOND**

1

Courageous constituent cohorts
commune, connect, conglomerate.
Confront conquest—commandos!
Collapse Confederate columns!
Codify common-compassion conduct codes!

Corrupt cops cordon corners,
corral coughing commoners.
Constitutional?
Cowardly!
Kooky conservative commentators
condone combustion,
contrive cognitive confusion,
conflate communistic collusion.
Cocky commanders
coddle conspiratorial consiglieri.

Consequence, consequences.

2

Corona contagion cowering collapses collectivity.
Contemplating conflictual contended contact?
Company coming?
Confer coffee, cola, Kombucha, coconut cobbler?
Coated cocoa cookies?
Cocktails cool cottonmouth.
Cook concocted confections.
Cozy conversation.
Could closeted copacetic colleagues come?
Could?

Eric Diamond is a psychotherapist, men's work leader, guitarist, and poet living in Gainesville since 1981. His first two books of poetry and lyrics are *Strange Frontier* and *Hold This Goblet*. Major influences on his work are Bob Dylan, Allen Ginsberg, and Robert Bly. He is the husband of noted local artist Jacquelyne Collett.

PANDEMIC PRIMARY: WHY I VOLUNTEERED AT A POLLING STATION DESPITE CORONAVIRUS*

» BY ZACHARIAH CHOU

When a primary takes place during a pandemic, civic duty clashes with social responsibility. Everybody should stay in. Everybody should vote.

My story begins on the Friday before the Tuesday [March 17, 2020] primary in Florida. I saw a post on Facebook that urged healthy people who could help out on Election Day to become poll workers. About 100 poll workers (probably older folks) in Alachua county, where I attend university, had dropped out due to coronavirus fears.

I'm twenty-two years old. I'm pretty healthy. I called the supervisor of elections office. One hour later, I was at the office undergoing deputy training. Deputies are the people who stand by the entrance telling people to take out their IDs and silence their phones. They keep the peace, which I suppose would be a lot easier not during a pandemic.

On Saturday, I was assigned to a precinct. On Monday, the clerk called me to tell me to be there Tuesday at 6 am and that she was bringing chicken soup. On Election Day, I loaded my own hand sanitizer, disinfecting wipes, and isopropyl alcohol into my backpack and headed to the church that would be my home for the next sixteen hours.

I was happy to see the supervisor of elections office had provided our site with ample hand sanitizer, hydrogen peroxide, paper towels, gloves, and even a spray bottle with alcohol.

My first job was putting up the "No Soliciting" sign, which state law mandates has to be 150 feet away from the entrance of the polling site. I was supplied with a 150-foot rope and set off, with one end on the door handle of the entrance. I really don't know how I managed to tangle the brand new rope as I unwrapped it, but I know that I will never feel as bad about tangling my headphones from now on.

Then we set up signs marking accessible parking, signs helping point people toward the entrance, signs telling people to turn off their phones, and so on.

When we opened at 7 am, there was a line of people who hoped to beat the crowd by coming early. As the day went on, some people came with gloves and masks. Others held their driver's licenses through plastic bags, napkins, and receipts. Several asked to use their own pens.

While posted outside, I propped open the doors to save voters from having to interact with one more "high-touch" surface. Every fifteen minutes, I sanitized the guardrails by the steps leading to the door.

POLLING STATION (PHOTO
BY ZACHARIAH CHOU)

After a moment of divine inspiration, I placed "I voted" stickers on the ground, six feet apart from each other, so when a line formed, it would conform to the principle of social distancing. Nothing says "social distancing" like spending your day interacting with almost 300 strangers, right?

Over the course of the day, I had four bowls of chicken soup and countless packets of fruit gummies. The people who passed through our polling site were grateful and thanked us for "risking it." They were jittery and cautious but also determined to cast their ballots. They were relieved when they saw that we were taking hygiene and social distancing seriously.

At final count, 280 people voted at our station before I closed the doors at 7 pm. We spent the next two hours cleaning up and completing paperwork.

There was a lot of pushback toward the State of Florida for holding elections during a pandemic as opposed to delaying them, like other states. It's hard to say if it was the right decision, as conditions may very well worsen in the future. But looking back on today, I am proud to have served as a poll worker. We did everything we could to mitigate risk to those who wanted to make their voices heard.

These are trying times that have tested everything that we used to take for granted. I don't think I'll ever see voting in the same light, now that I've seen all the people who put in countless hours and, in this election, put their health at risk in order to keep a polling location open.

*This essay originally appeared in *The Guardian* on April 22, 2020.

Zachariah Chou was born and raised in Pembroke Pines, FL. He came to the University of Florida and graduated with degrees in political science and journalism. While at UF he was an active part of Student Government and afterwards served as the opinions editor of *The Independent Florida Alligator*. He also worked at the Bob Graham Center for Public Service as a student assistant, helping out with their numerous civic engagement efforts.

FLASHBACK AND FLASHPOINT: FURY OVER INJUSTICE

» **BY RONNIE LOVLER**

Today I am experiencing the same feelings of discord, dissonance, and social disarray that I did twice before. Once was in 1967, when my hometown of Newark, New Jersey, erupted in riots, provoked then as now by episodes of racial injustice. The other was in 1970, while a student at Ohio State University, during the national anti-Vietnam War campus protests.

Back then I felt disconcerted and distressed by what was happening, exactly as I do today about what is happening now.

In Newark, the inciting incident was white police officers' arrest of an African-American man. The Newark riots were a culmination point in what subsequently became known as the "long hot summer of 1967," a reference to the 159 riots that erupted in cities across the United States that summer.

When I was nineteen years old, home from university for the summer, unrest was simmering all over the city. My neighborhood in the Weequahic section of Newark was once predominantly, almost exclusively, Jewish. By that summer, that was no longer the case.

My neighborhood had a new look. Jackie, who lived across the street and was always with his German shepherd, Caesar, was gone. A Black family was living there now. Joey next door was gone, so was Irene across the street. My neighborhood now had a racially diverse face.

I can't lay any familial claim to standing up for social justice. My father would have moved us in a heartbeat. But he couldn't find a buyer for our home and we didn't have the money for the double jeopardy of paying two mortgages or one mortgage and a rent.

What this meant was that, unlike many of my high school friends whose families had moved to the suburbs, I got to live in an integrated and racially diverse neighborhood. While home for the summer, I became accustomed to seeing faces of many colors in my neighborhood, and hence in my life.

When the riots broke out in downtown Newark, I was eager to witness what was happening with my own eyes. The fledging journalist that I was wanted to be there. Needless to say, I did not even get close. I ranted and raved, but my father stood firm and said that his daughter was not going anywhere near downtown Newark.

I was glued to the TV. I listened to radio news updates. I consumed our local newspapers, the morning *Newark Star Ledger* and the afternoon *Newark Evening News*. And then it was over, and it was over for me, too. I went back to my summer economics class. I went back to going down to the shore on the weekends. I went back to my boyfriend.

The disturbances did not spur me on to activism. I returned to life as a good "liberal," supporting the right causes, but without becoming involved enough to make change happen. I thought if I was a journalist, my telling of the stories was my way to contribute.

So I continued my studies at Ohio State University. It wasn't until my last year of school that I became marginally involved with the anti-Vietnam War protest movement on my campus.

I shared a home for a while with Chris, another journalism student, and her boyfriend, who was a Vietnam War vet and a leader of the Columbus chapter of Viet Vets Against the War.

On April 30, 1970, President Nixon announced the expansion of the Vietnam War into Cambodia. On May 1, massive protests began around the country on college campuses and different cities. Ohio State was no exception. We marched and we chanted slogans like *"Peace Now! Peace Now!"* or *"Stop the Bombing! Stop the War!"* or *"One, two, three, four, We don't want your f.....g war."*

Nominally, I was also part of the Ohio State anti-war "leadership" team, with my little Honda 50cc motor scooter. My role was to "scoot" around campus and see how the different marches were faring and report back.

On May 4, during another protest at Kent State University, National Guardsmen called to the campus shot and killed four students and injured ten others. The shots were heard around the country.

In Columbus, that day, I had joined a protest at the Oval, a huge grassy lawn, then and now a classic meet-up place at Ohio State, when we heard about what had happened at Kent State. We ran into an open classroom building and took shelter there. We weren't sure from what, but we were upset and we were frightened.

We ventured out a few hours later to learn that a nationwide student strike was underway. It would last for days and involve millions of students, including me.

In any case, the protests and demonstrations of today triggered by the police killing of George Floyd gave me pause to reflect on my own experiences. In 1967 Newark, five days of looting and arson left twenty-six people dead and tens of millions of dollars in damages. It also made Newark a buzzword for blight and urban decay for decades.

As far as Vietnam, we all know the outcome. The United States withdrew, airlifting the last remaining Americans out of Saigon on April 30, 1975. Vietnam unified and today is thriving.

Newark has progressed and has learned to protest peacefully and effectively, certainly at the time of this writing. In an interview with *The New York Times*, Newark Mayor Ras Baraka noted, "A lot of tension. A lot of anxiety. But the community held the line."

Now what happened in Newark is spreading across the country. The latest wave of protests has been massive and mostly peaceful. Silence is not golden and protest can prompt change, but we also need good leadership. A different president might have put forth a message of hope and healing instead of words that divided us even more. We just voted for change and maybe, just maybe, now things will get better.

A MURAL IN SOUTHEAST GAINESVILLE HONORS
THE LIFE OF BREANNA TAYLOR, WHO WAS SHOT IN
HER HOME BY POLICE IN LOUISVILLE, KY IN MARCH,
2020 (PHOTO BY MICHAEL TAPIA LOVLER)

IN OTHER NEWS...

» BY K. E. MULLINS

COVID is the news. It isn't to me. Yet, that's all they covered on T.V. Is there no weather? Oh yeah, they report that.

Murder has stopped and crime is at an all-time low. Is that so? Hell no...and rape. Well, we'll talk about that at eight.

Did the election stop? I guess. But, not. That's what they want you to believe. Conceive. Only thing to listen to is the COVID. Nineteen. Is that nineteen cases or is it for 2019? This is the real mystery.

In Other News...

There is no other news. My bad there is the death rate. Today, New York City is at an all-time low. Louisiana is reaching its peak and California. It's still a mystery to me. And Georgia, let's not go there. They will be doing hair, Friday. So, buyer beware.

What were we saying...Oh yeah! In Other News...

Florida is open. The beaches, that is. COVID up or down? The rate is climbing and it's still hot. While the death rate is not.

K. E. Mullins is a Florida native. She began her writing career while in the U. S. Navy by venturing into poetry. Her poem, "My One Last Cent," was published in *Amistad,* a literary journal at Howard University. Currently, Ms. Mullins has self-published a book of poetry, *Thinking Aloud: Dimensions of Free-Verse,* and her fiction novels, *The Friends and Family Connection: Get Unplugged, In the Company of Strangers*, and *Murder: Another Name for Revenge.* She is also a regular contributor to *Harness* magazine.

FLORIDA PRESIDENTIAL PRIMARY ELECTION

» **BY MICHAEL PLAUT**

Being a precinct clerk is a little like being a flight attendant. There are lots of things you have to know and there are many procedures to follow, often detailed and exacting ones. But the real test of a precinct clerk and his or her staff is how well they handle the unusual things that come up in any election—voters needing special assistance of some kind, ambiguous ballots that cannot be scanned, address changes, voter confusion, equipment failures, etc. As on a commercial flight, these things are not necessarily frequent, but one must be prepared for them.

In this case, we had another layer of challenge—a highly contagious viral infection sweeping much of the world, little knowledge about how to address that challenge, and a fair amount of anxiety among some people, including many of our trained poll workers. All of the poll workers go through mandatory training at the election office, and this must be done for every election, no matter how much experience one has. There are always new laws, regulations or procedures, and it is easy to forget things from one election to the next. For example, for this election, we were using Spanish language ballots for the first time, and the distance from the polling place that people could solicit voters had increased substantially. Rules for use of cameras in the polling place had changed as well.

On Monday, March 16th, I headed to the election office to pick up my supplies for the next day's election. As is typical, we went through each item, checked it off, and signed for it. This time, there were a few additional items in our large zippered bag—gloves, wipes, screen cleaners, bottles of disinfectant, and paper towels. I went home and reexamined everything and contacted the eight people on my precinct staff one last time to make sure they were working. All were still on board except two. My assistant clerk had been reassigned as a clerk in a precinct that had lost a clerk. My ballot scanner decided she did not want to risk exposure in a public setting.

Late Monday afternoon, I kept an appointment at Precinct 54—the Florida Museum of Natural History at the University of Florida—to make sure that our large locked cart of supplies and our two ballot scanners had arrived and were securely locked away, to check the phone connection for transmitting our data after polls closed, and also to instruct the museum staff as to how I wanted the polling room to be set up. I had prepared a diagram ahead of time, as always.

Then, a well-earned good night's sleep. I had to be at the museum at 5:30 am.

When we started setting up for the election at 6:00 am, I was missing three of my eight staff, one of my three EViD computer operators, my ballot scanner, and my assistant clerk. I later learned that was not unusual on that particular day. Fortunately, the election office had trained a large number of back-up people and by the time the polls opened, I had my third EViD operator and a ballot scanner. The office went through four possibilities before I finally got a scanner, but he was great. I never did have an assistant clerk.

While a few of us got our scanners and supplies out of locked storage with the aid of the museum's security personnel, everyone else started sanitizing all the tables and chairs in the room. We then had our usual job of putting up signs, booting up our equipment, and setting up voting booths and ballot pens. Without an assistant clerk or ballot scanner for a while, I booted up both scanners on my own, something normally done by two people. Our deputy was a first timer, so she needed some guidance as well. While we normally try to be ready to open polls by 6:30, it was 6:50 when we were ready for our 7:00 am opening. Whew!

The day went smoothly, with no major problems. Voters were good about spacing themselves in line. We processed about 275 voters at our precinct, a comfortable level. People subbed for each other during breaks. The museum staff was helpful when needed, and the election office was very responsive when we had questions or problems. We had our usual number of student address changes, and it is so nice that we can do that quickly over the phone if they are transferring from another county in Florida. As usual, a few voters were unhappy that they could not vote for presidential candidates, but Florida is a closed primary state, and if you are not registered with a political party, you cannot vote for partisan candidates in a primary election. The office does try to inform voters in advance of that fact, but....

We had a bit of a crunch after the polls closed, and this is where the absence of an assistant clerk was really felt. One of our ballot scanners crashed when we attempted transmit data, so I had to go to the room where the transfer was being made and reboot the scanner with help from the office. Once the machine was again up and running, the transmission went well.

I then had the job of reconciling the number of ballots used with the number of ballots cast, and that is ultimately the most important job of the clerk—accounting for all of the ballots. I always try to compare figures throughout the day so I can identify problems soon after they occur. Some ballots may be spoiled for some reason, or unscanned, and we have provisional ballots to account for as well. Fortunately, it all worked out, but it was about 8:30 pm when we were finally able to leave the polling place. One poll worker had to accompany me to the office to turn in our ballots and other documents, as is required. It was after 9:30 pm when I finally arrived home.

All in all, it was a good day at Precinct 54. I cannot tell what our voter count might have been if the COVID threat had not been with us, but other than the shortage of staff, and with the help of a very conscientious crew of poll workers, and good support from the office, we made it!

Dr. Michael Plaut is a seventy-nine year old retired psychologist. He served most of his career on the faculty of the University of Maryland School of Medicine, both in the Department of Psychiatry and as Assistant Dean for Student Affairs. He has been married to his wife, Judy, for fifty-two years. She is a graduate of the University of Florida. They have been residents of Oak Hammock at the University of Florida since 2013.

IN VIRUS TIME

» **BY LESLIE SAHLER**

In virus time
between sleep

and sleep
I ease my labor

of forty-two years.
This flame

of aliveness
is my secret treasure.

Behind my heart,
an abiding heart speaks.

Leslie Sahler has lived in and around Gainesville since 1981 and works, semi-retired, as a clinical social worker/therapist.

INTERVIEW WITH DR. KAYSER ENNEKING, MD

» **INTERVIEW WITH DR. KAYSER ENNEKING, MD (CONDUCTED BY RONNIE LOVLER, MATHESON HISTORY MUSEUM, DECEMBER 7, 2020)**

Ronnie Lovler: You commented on how good it was that Joe Biden won the election, irrespective of the outcome for your race.

Kayser Enneking: I really wanted to win my race to represent District 21 in the Florida House, but for me personally, and for the country, I think it was really important that Joe Biden win, and I was very proud of the work that we were able to do to help make that happen, even though he didn't win Florida. And even though whatever we might have contributed was very small, I still felt like we did our part. That was essential work that needed to be done.

I probably won't run for office again. What I realized, and Bennett realized, because I had run for office in 2018, and to turn around and run another campaign in 2020, was a big chunk of my life that I spent doing that. And I needed to get sort of reoriented to what my real life was.

RL: How did COVID impact you and the people you served or hoped to serve?

KE: COVID in its own weird way, made it more difficult. Because it injected so much uncertainty in how we could campaign, and what was safe to do and what was responsible to do, and that just added to the anxiety level of what we had.

Not only were we anxious about my work and being exposed at work and worried about it for both of our families, but also we were worried about our volunteers and our staff workers and just trying to make sure that we were responsible. Almost every week we said, should we be doing something different? Should we be knocking on doors? Should we be trying to do more in-person stuff? And every week the answer was still no, it just wasn't the responsible thing to do.

COVID has devastated many communities around the country. I think that we have been relatively fortunate here in Alachua County and in Gilchrist and Dixie, counties where I would have been the representative, in the sense that we just were a little bit out of sync with all the other issues when they arose. So for instance, in Florida, we had our big spike in the summer, which I attributed to the fact that everybody went indoors. It's hot in the summer and everybody stays indoors.

Our city government, our county government was very responsible early on, making sure that people were wearing masks, and I think that really helped us as the pandemic went on.

You know, one of the things that I think Ben and I were really most proud about our campaign was that we were able to use the platform that we had, a campaign platform to be able to tap into my expertise in modern medicine and science.

And in terms of my ability to interpret that for lay people so that we could tell them sort of what we knew, what we didn't know, and what we think the best evidence is. So early on, we were advocating wearing masks, washing your hands, socially distancing, gosh, it turns out that those were all really good things.

That was probably the best thing about our campaign, that we really could become a source of truth for people about COVID, and I was very proud of that work. We did twenty-two different webinars around COVID during the campaign.

I think it was very helpful. That was probably the best use of my time to help our community during the campaign.

RL: Can you provide a specific example, or examples in the plural, of how COVID made things more difficult for you?

KE: As a person, as a physician, or as a candidate?

RL: In all ways.

KE: COVID is such a new disease process, I think there was this incredible level of anxiety in our country. Some of it was exacerbated by the political tension around COVID. That made it so you were either in the believer camp and you were afraid of it, or you are in the non-believer camp and thought it was a hoax.

And so I think in all three parts of my life, it just created this level of uncertainty and anxiety that made it a strain to do any one of those jobs well.

Bennett Ragan: We did twenty-two virtual town halls, and it is one of the things I'm most proud of that we were able to accomplish. And Kayser had touched on this, the way that we thought about what was safe and what wasn't safe.

We ran a political campaign for fourteen months during a pandemic and not a single staffer, volunteer, or intern or anybody like that got sick. And I think that is something that I'm really proud of, as the manager.

I know that a large number of campaigns throughout Florida had COVID cases and to not be part of that and not put people in harm's way is important.

KE: And throw in that I was still going to the hospital and being exposed to all kinds of people, and yet we still were able to make it so that neither I nor anybody else got sick or made anybody else sick.

RL: What new methods or skills did you develop that might carry over to post-COVID times?

KE: I think we all got much more familiar with these technologies that allow us to interact in a in a more virtual way. It did take me a while to learn how to do it and to be engaging. A lot of politics is theater. When I first ran, I thought politics was all about ideas, and I thought the person who had the better idea was the person who won. But it turns out that leaders, and what people look for in political leaders, is a whole lot more complicated than just that. And so, to a certain extent it's theater that's involved in making sure that you express your ideas in a way that is welcoming, and it's sort of meeting people where they are, and that it's not off-putting.

So, for me, because people know I have a bunch of degrees, the pictures behind me are of my kids. So people understand that I have a family and that I am every bit as proud of that as of any degree that I can have on my wall.

RL: And on the personal side?

KE: There were two people that I really was worried about getting COVID. One was my son who is diabetic and one is my 93-year-old mother-in-law, who is living with us, and both of them got it.

And so personally, I was extraordinarily worried about people that I know and love, so I probably campaigned on that with a passion that I think it deserves. But it was a passion that really came from my heart.

RL: Everybody is okay now?

KE: Everybody has recovered. But we do not know the long-term effects of COVID. But will there be any subsequent effects of it? I don't know that anybody knows yet.

RL: What else did you gain from your COVID experience?

BR: This was a really interesting opportunity to be working as a campaign manager because there's no playbook for running a campaign during a pandemic. What you know to keep people safe was the exact opposite of what you want to do in a campaign, to limit your interactions with people, limit your person-to-person contacts.

And that's the antithesis of good campaigning. Usually you want to get in front of people, shaking their hands, and making sure that they understand that you have the right ideas for the job. But you also want to connect with them on a human level.

We cut out all of our person-to-person events and contacts. That was a conscious decision on my part. I think that we still did a fantastic job of reaching people. We made 83,000 phone calls and sent 55,000 text messages. So it's not like we didn't connect with people.

We ran an extremely competitive paid communications program that was unrivaled by most of our peers.

And we were not able to get it across the finish line.

And I think that there's a lot to be said for the fact that our opponent, and many of the opponents on the other side of the aisle, the Republican Party, were not nearly as safe as we were. ... Many of their campaigns had multiple staff infections of COVID. ...They were knocking on doors and they were talking to people. And I don't know if we can really say that that's why they won. I just think that's irresponsible.

But, the digital pivot was tough. I think it was tough for a lot of candidates, you know. Kayser is really great digitally, and she's very engaging.

KE: I think people and the voters were tired by November 3. They were tired of COVID. They were tired of being told what to do. They were tired of wearing masks. They were tired of being isolated, just like everybody, and I think to some extent, some of the success that the Republicans had down ballot was because their message was, it's not really that big of a deal, the Democrats are weenies, they're scaredy cats.

But it wasn't the responsible thing to do. And if that's what it takes to win an election, to be irresponsible, then I think we're in trouble in this country.

BR: I think that a lot of people wanted to hear a more inspirational message. It's going to be fine. And I think that the Republican message of let's just gets back to normal, and so be it, some people are going to die. I think that's morally wrong. I think that actually one of the hardest parts about this post-election, post-mortem process is that I would not have changed what we did, because I think it was the morally right thing to do.

RL: Again, how did COVID get in the way of your campaign?

KE: I couldn't kiss babies! I did actually run two different campaigns one in COVID and one not. And the thing that I loved about campaigning in person was kissing babies and connecting with people … and talking to little kids and explaining to them what it was I was doing and why I was doing it. It is an honor to get to talk to people, and what they see that they could do with their lives, and how you can help them get there, and coronavirus just made it so that that really wasn't possible and that, I truly, truly, truly missed.

BR: I think on a practical management side was the way that coronavirus impacted fundraising. We did go through quite a significant lull in our fundraising at the peak of the pandemic, and that impacted our ability to build up our organization at an earlier date.

So actually, a really significant impact of COVID on our organization was the dip in fundraising and the way that that impacted our ability to expand the campaign.

KE: About March 7, when we began to realize that this was truly happening, I went back to work full time for a couple of weeks. So I spent the first two weeks of that, canceling cases for people that were very frail, and that morphed into canceling all surgical cases that were not urgent or emergent. I had to parse through all of the different cases; we cancelled almost 5,000 cases and had to kind of go through each one of them individually. … I had a lot of help doing it, but that was sort of my job at the hospital for about a month, and so campaigning was gone; I had a much more important thing to do. It was such an unusual and uncomfortable time for everybody. The last thing people wanted was for me to call them and ask them for money. So I was like, not only am I busy, but also I am not going to do that. … Did that come back to bite us? Maybe, but it was still the right thing to do.

RL: How did COVID make it more difficult to get your message out, particularly in terms of canvassing?

KE: With canvassing you get the opportunity to say what issues are important to you. Over time, it really helps to massage your message. It's what people want to talk about.

And instead, because we didn't get that feedback, we didn't get a chance to really change our messaging or make our messaging more nuanced towards what people wanted to talk about. So canvassing turns out to be really important, not just for the kind of one-on-one interaction that you get, but also for sort of the Gestalt that you get about a community, and that's a really important thing that perhaps I didn't appreciate as much before all this.

BR: I think we probably missed some cues that we may have picked up on as far as what was important. We would have contacted significantly more people if we had been knocking on doors. It's just kind of the way it works.

People don't like to answer their phones anymore. We all know the barrage of robo calls we get on a daily basis. … Canvassing is a tried and true way of reaching people. It's obvious that text messages and phone calls are just not nearly as effective.

KE: The other thing is in-person things where people can stand up and ask you questions. I think that's an incredibly important opportunity for people who are running for office, particularly if you're not an incumbent. The person that I ran against strategically didn't show up for anything.

… I think that's a red light flashing for democracy that you can still get elected with that kind of behavior.

BR: That places significantly larger emphasis on paid communications, versus earned media or non-paid communications that you get from doing outreach. And that caused our campaign, like many other campaigns, to spend much more time fundraising in order to fund those paid communications.

KE: One thing that was really very interesting about doing a zoom event versus an in-person event was, I thought people asked me harder questions. I'd give my little spiel. And then I'd say, does anybody have a question and the questions that they asked tended to be just harder to answer.

Because they weren't going to see me over the cheese ball after the question and answer things, they felt it was okay to ask much more pointed, harder questions, and I found that to be fascinating and that was completely consistent with every event that we had.

RL: Anything else you would like to add?

KE: I think it is wonderful that you guys are doing this, because you know the saying is, you are lucky if you live in interesting times. Well, we are living in interesting times. And I think because we're still sort of in the midst of it, we don't even realize how abnormal it is. People ten, twenty years from now will have no idea how abnormal this was.

THE INFERNAL DIN OF OUR DILEMMA

» BY ERIC DIAMOND

Dilemma: a situation in which a difficult choice has to be made between two or more alternatives, especially equally undesirable ones.

"Somehow, we've reached the point where caring about public health has become a progressive issue, while the nation's economy has become a conservative one. This division is false; no one should have to choose between financial annihilation and helping to spread a deadly disease"

– K. Landman

Icarus escaped Daedalus' maze, only to crash headlong
into the sea. Leaders, supply all hospitals in full,
just for shits and grins—this is your dilemma!

No longer just air, but aerosol. Every cough is a nervous cough.
Our defense is porous, terror's in the backfield. Draft Jimmy Vaccine
in Round One, we need to win now! Bad season, this dilemma.

On a simple errand, Salah encountered the bony finger of
Death in the marketplace. Run to your Master, mount his donkey,
fly to Samarra, flee your fateful run-in with the dilemma.

Virus, you are Einsatzgruppen, lung-munching Lecters
arcing an exponential vector. Mocking logic in hot spots, and
lurking in radioactive laundry bins in the hallways of our dilemma.

Viral virago, bounding from bats, camels, birds, to helpless
homo sapiens. One law: that of the jungle. Feel the heated breath
of the lions, leaning in to the sweaty threat of our dilemma.

In Vegas, pikers pull levers in lobbies and airports, watching
spinners with the giddy hope of the damned. Cherries and
dollar signs revolve, but you're always done in, in this dilemma.

Spry grandmas become cipher-ghosts boxed for open graves.
Either you beseech the deafened gods, or drink blame-fever bleach.
At the witch trials, the verdicts are in: death by dilemma.

Tumbleweeds wend down empty streets, ambling toward
unmoved mountains. The peaks are bathed in clear light.
Wizened sheriff, with your rusty badge of tin, arrest this dilemma.

Masked messengers of God, wail your lonesome Kaddish,
your green-black benedictions. Dark is the night, when the
Holy Ones drown from within. Damn, damn this dilemma.

The moonshiners are pouring in the gulley behind Carter's farm.
The regulars complain: "you call this railroad gin?
Triple the strength, before its last call"—the fix is in on this dilemma.

On the ship of fools, they keep the gutting hooks close at hand.
The captain wipes blood on his nautical charts. The plank
extends leeward. Prepare to swim with shark fins, condemned to dilemma.

The accountant's desk is stained with red ink. The ledgers
are lopsided, crazy packs of zeroes bubble out, while merchandise
rots from neglect. All the clients want aspirin, for this nasty dilemma.

The shattering, the blistering, the mad rush, the razor's edge,
the tuberous nails welding the ventilator crucifix. The
sweat patina on moldering untouched skin. Do not touch the dilemma.

Can there be poetry after COVID? Mere street noise may wound
the cochlea. Can there be comedy, or barbershop quartets?
Choirs of angels? Or only the infernal din of our dilemma?

Eric, guard your health well. Amalek preys on the caravan,
plucking laggards off the rear columns. Many a gust of wind
is needed to stay airborne, on the flak-pocked wings of our dilemma.

CHAPTER 6

PHILOSOPHICAL AND PSYCHOLOGICAL REACTIONS

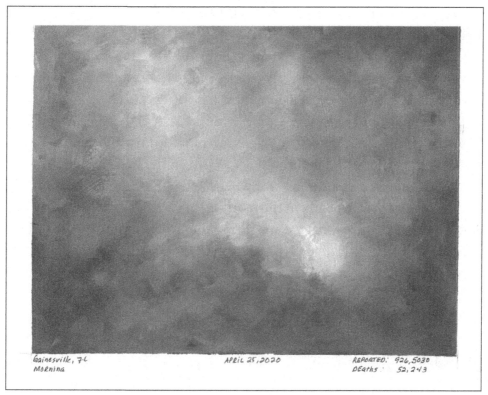

APRIL 25, 2020 (GWENDOLYN CHRZANOWSKI)

WHAT TO BE THANKFUL FOR DURING THIS TIME OF PANDEMIC

» **BY ROSEMARIE DINKLAGE**

When the Russians invaded Germany in 1945, I was 6 ½ years old. My mother decided to flee from the eastern part of Germany to the western part, which became West Germany in 1948. We left on the very last train; it had 110 cars, two locomotives pulling, and one pushing.

My aunt and family lived in the same town. My uncle was a butcher and did not have to become a soldier. They decided to stay. The Russians shot all the men who stayed behind. My uncle was shot in front of my aunt and their two children. Women and children were expelled; they had one hour to leave the house and town. The baby was born in a hospital in Berlin but died of starvation a short time afterwards. My aunt could not produce milk and there was none to buy. One of my uncles, my mother's brother, died in Siberia.

Eventually, the five of us lived in a guest house for ten years. We had two rooms. One was the bedroom for us four kids, ages 15, 6 ½, 4, and 1 ½. It had two beds, one head south and one head north. The other became the living room for my mother (she slept on the sofa), kitchen, dining room, and bathroom. I was fifteen the first time I took a shower or bath. There were many times after the war when we had nothing to eat. In the summer, my mother and older sister left early in the morning to gather berries for breakfast, lunch, and dinner. I don't remember what we ate during the winter months. I don't think I ever really felt deprived, other than of food, and I enjoyed my childhood picking berries, gathering mushrooms, going cross-country skiing, having snowball fights, attending outdoor concerts. It was horrible for my mother and my older sister.

My father was a soldier in Normandy, France, and became an American prisoner of war. They made him a cook because he was a baker. We had a bakery and my aunt and uncle had a butcher shop, so plenty to eat during the war. My parents divorced when I was ten years old.

When COVID-19 arrived, I made a list of all the positive things in my life:

I have a beautiful home, food in the refrigerator/freezer/kitchen cabinets, money for shopping and paying my bills, friends and family to call. I also have a television to watch operas, listen to concerts around the world, and see travel programs, just to give a few examples. I also earned my Ph.D. in this country. I have time to read, eat, and write. Unfortunately, eating became a priority and I gained around fifteen pounds.

In January, Everfield Press published my dual book called *My Name is Schnuckiputz: Just call me Schnucki*, illustrated by Inge Cibis who lives in Germany. One book is a Picture Book and one is a Reader which comes with either colorful illustrations or in black and white. The book is an interactive children's story designed to encourage positive conversations between a child and parent or caregiver. The Picture Book has been translated into Spanish and German. The German version of the Reader is currently being edited in Germany.

I saw friends every morning at the pool. We respected social distancing. We discussed various subjects, from politics to possible hurricanes, storms, the fires in California, what charity to help financially, whether we should get our teeth cleaned, and what store has specials. Two neighbors and their friends play classical music in the morning once a week. We also started a book club, calling ourselves the Bookettes, and decided to read relatively short and happy books. Well, the first one was *Mice and Men* by Steinbeck. It met the criteria of short, but not happy.

What helps me tremendously is seeing friends from my Children's Book Pod and Writers Alliance, usually on Zoom. All are positive, caring, and encouraging. I started to see other friends for lunch or dinner, as long as the restaurants serve food outdoors.

I take a drive once a week or so to see the countryside and not just the grocery stores.

I am a member of the Unitarian Universalist Fellowship of Gainesville. We meet on Zoom to listen to the service and are reminded of our obligations to be compassionate in human relations, respect for the interdependent web of all existence of which we are a part, and the goal of world community with peace, liberty, and justice for all, just to name a few of the principles. This helps me to divert my thinking from myself to my surroundings close by and world-wide.

It gets lonely at times, and I wish I could travel again. I love seeing how people live in other parts of the world. I envy people who have family around, either they live with them or, better still, can visit with them, even with masks and social distancing. But then there are families who have little or no money because of illness, loss of jobs, lack of education, or just plain different skin color or sexual orientation. I feel sorry for people who have to evacuate their homes because of fires, flooding, etc. These people might never be able to return, because nothing is left. When this happens, I remind myself of the things to be grateful for.

Now that it is cooler and we are no longer meeting at the pool on a regular basis, I have to find new outlets to socialize. I am 82 years old, widowed, and I am wondering how long I have to wait until I can see family and friends again and taste that wonderful German food.

Rosemarie Dinklage was born in Reppen, east of Berlin. When Russian soldiers entered Germany in 1945, she was six. Her family fled toward the west. In January, 1959, she went to England, via Paris, as an au-pair. In 1960, at age twenty-two, she came to New York to see the Big Apple and America and worked as a bilingual secretary. Later, she received her B.A. and M.A. and, upon her husband's death, came to Gainesville to obtain her Ph.D. She worked as a school psychologist for many years, is now retired and lives with her dog, Cloe.

QUARANTINED

» **BY E. STANLEY RICHARDSON**

the other day
a group of us
... quarantined

ventured out
to stroll
down

anytown
main street
USA

standing
six feet
abreast
... cautiously
across
the ghostly
thoroughfare

no longer teeming
unrecognizable
... in our absence

it looked more like
an
eerie
... abandoned
movie set

the youngest among us
pondered
... aloud

is this for real
when will we
awaken
from this
dream

tomorrow perhaps
or
the day after the day
after
the day
after

then
we'll have
brunch
... downtown
with
a multitude of
friends
.. in the evening
we'll have an early
dinner
at
our favorite
spot
... afterwards
absorb
a
musical
at the
... vibrant
theater

and we'll sit

.. undaunted

side by
side
by

beautiful
side

Quarantined #2

between us

everywhere there is
distance

even lovers
are
reluctant
afraid
to embrace

we flee from
touch

to breathe
too deeply

parents
grand parents
hesitate
to snuggle
their children

the handshake has been
outlawed

to hug is
death

that is the penalty

isolation

yesterday I drove to the graveyard
to hold tight
the living

I needed to
feel

my ancestor's
arms

around me.

Quarantined #3

we still go
for walks

but

the walks
are different now
the cadence struts
more
deliberate

giving attention to
its rhythm

our eyes
brighter

even the breeze

the texture of
trees
the color of
leaves

the bird's song
amplified

how the different houses
lean

things left out front
on the lawn

our journey
now

vivid

alive
with feeling

much more
blessed

since
our neighbor's

untimely
departure

E. Stanley Richardson is an American poet, actor, playwright, social/political commentator and lecturer. The inaugural Poet Laureate of Alachua County, Florida (2020-2022), he is the author of the award winning book of poetry, *Hip Hop Is Dead - Long Live Hip Hop: The Birth, Death and Resurrection of Hip Hop Activism* (2017). He is the Founder/Director of ARTSPEAKSgnv: "Bringing Poetry & People Together," as well as the Director of the Alachua County/North Central Florida Youth Poet Laureate Program. E. Stanley Richardson is a Florida native and currently resides in Alachua County, Florida.

THE ANTITHESIS OF COVID-19

» BY KAREN COLE-SMITH

While on the surface, many have discussed at length all of the negative outcomes and consequences associated with COVID-19, and there are many too devastating to confront or even comprehend, for me and, I am sure, others, many blessings have resulted out of this pandemic. It has certainly given me more time to meditate daily and be more grateful for all of the things I have, i.e. my husband, family, friends, social partners, and community that continue to thrive in spite of it. They've always been important, but staying connected with them is now given a greater priority than ever before, and being concerned about their well-being is number one on my list.

I've even done a "baptism by fire" training on as many technology training programs and apps as possible, so that I can remain in touch and survive. This was something that I thought was beyond my reach, and now it's something that I have mastered because these persons and my community are so important to me. I've also taken a lot more time to read in depth on health-related topics and books, and I am eating more nutritiously. I know the importance of having this knowledge, changing some behaviors, and knowing how it will impact me, my family, friends, and community in the long run, especially the African American community, which has been so heavily impacted, and of which I am a part.

The hardest part has been threefold: as a sociologist/criminologist, the lack of personal interaction and communication has been difficult. This field of study focuses heavily on social connections, so adjusting to social distancing has been a task, but having more time for research has been a blessing.

Secondly, as an only child whose mother lives five hours away in a county that is dealing with serious COVID-19 issues, and knowing that I can't reach her physically, has been difficult. I have always been there with my mom, who is quickly approaching ninety, on Mother's Day. This will be the first time in thirty-five plus years I won't be "at her feet or in her presence" and feel her touch and look into her beautiful eyes and physically see her smile. That will be most difficult for me. (So glad I've learned to use some of the technology apps recently and I can see her on Face Time!)

The third greatest challenge has been job related, since it deals with community outreach efforts and working with the East Gainesville community. While some conversations and partnering can continue via Zoom, Teams, Canvas, and other computer-related techniques, building communities and strengthening outreach, in my view, requires hands on, face to face interaction and conversations. Holding a hand with someone in the community, listening directly, and letting persons know that what they say matters, and that you are there for them, is important.

So these are challenges that I will have to deal with and confront, with no timeline for when things will change. These timelines and uncertainties of COVID-19 are not something that I have control over and are in the hands of a higher power. I must admit that I have cried some tears when I see long lines for food and resources and listen to stories of those who are lacking the things that I have always taken for granted.

And yet, out of all of this, I go back to my beginning statement. Just when I thought that nothing good could come out this for me, and all of its negative implications with no end in sight, it's been positive in more ways than one. I now have more family time, more time to meditate, more time to be grateful, more time to read and become more educated in areas that I never had time for before, more time to do personal check-ins on the elderly at my church and in the community, more time to make home-cooked meals, and most importantly, more time to pray more than once a day. A pastor on the internet recently stated during his sermon that while many things have been cancelled, gratitude ain't cancelled. So during this season, I will continuously remind myself that we still have a lot to be grateful for, and we should take the time during the social distancing period to do just that. Be grateful. I will. Amen.

Dr. Karen Cole-Smith is currently the executive director of Community Outreach and East Gainesville Initiative at Santa Fe College, where she has served for more than three decades. In this role, the college partners with community members and faith-based leaders to address gaps and inequities in education, workforce development, literacy, and technology, in efforts to bridge the digital divide. Growing up in South Florida, she has lived in North Central for the past thirty-five years. Her personal mission remains the same as outlined in the book of Micah: "to do justice, love kindness (mercy), and to walk humbly with my God."

THE GLOWERING BELLS

» **BY ERIC DIAMOND**

I so disdain the dull ring in my ears
A death-knell, glowering from the hills
Brother, I'm naught but the sum of my fears
And the doldrums, the shivers, the chills---

For it's Grandmama down with the plague now
And Uncle's been wracked with the cough
Rue the Devil, taking his curtsy and bow
All angel wings, curled and sloughed off—

Columns of beggars are pegged to the road
Crusts of bread and stone soup for the weary
Plow-handle's cracked, bitter seeds have been sowed
We beg mercy, from Jesus, and from Mary—

Whence comes end-times for these shadows?
Could clear paths appear on the morrow?
The germ's had its run of the meadows
And the trees are bent double with sorrow

ON ISOLATION

» **BY JAMES WILLIAMS**

Like most of us, I didn't take social isolation seriously until one friend put the kibosh on our weekly dinners. "You're the only friend I have who's in the high risk age range," she told me. This was an insult, I thought at first, but I couldn't deny she was absolutely right about the age range, and when I thought about it, I realized I was in several high risk categories due in part to a collapsed lung many years ago.

So, I went into seclusion, but being a writer, it didn't seem all that different from daily living. I had had a housemate for the prior six or eight months, but after isolation set in, she moved in with a new girlfriend. The house was again all mine. I was also trying to wrap up a book of short stories and I was getting them ready to self-publish. For that reason, the more or less enforced isolation was beneficial.

My next door neighbor gave me a medical mask, when I picked up a dozen eggs for his family as long as I was going to the grocery. The mask, in and of itself, took on its own significance and made the coronavirus real to me. It is not overstating the case to say that, walking around in public while wearing it, was a bit like coming out as a homosexual: see everybody, I'm in a high-risk category and I don't care who knows it.

I shaved my beard off, not from fear of infection so much as avoiding the wild-eyed hermetic look that was developing. The only otherwise unusual thing I've done that was noteworthy during isolation is that I streamed Wagner's entire Ring Cycle, because I had never seen a Wagnerian opera and it had been on my bucket list for years. I can't say I was consistently engrossed in all fifteen hours of it, but it taught me a lot about opera, about Wagner, and about contemporary American politics. I suspect this is a floodgate point for high and low culture, so far as media usage is concerned. Even I have had Zoom meetings with siblings and my Rotary Club for the first time and now expect to have more in the future, social isolation or not.

I go out some, when absolutely necessary, but before isolation I was in the grocery store two or three times a week. I have always carried a hand-held basket at the grocery store; I don't buy enough at one time to make a pushable buggy useful. While in isolation, I've continued to do so. But now, I'm in the store only two or three times a month, still buying no more at a time than I can carry in the same basket. And what do I need to learn from that? I will make it through two months or even a year of isolation, if necessary.

But it did hit me that if I contracted the virus within the next few weeks or months, those dearest friends and family members I can't wait to see again in person when this is over, I might already have seen for the last time. It has happened to others, it could happen to me. Now there's motivation for me. Let's just hope my temperate level of isolation is going to be enough.

James Williams was born at Alachua County Hospital in 1946, though his parents lived in a nearby county. He graduated from Gainesville High in 1963 and briefly attended the University of Florida before entering the Vietnam-era military. After living in Kansas, Boston, New York City, Shanghai, and Bradford County as an adult, he returned to Gainesville in 2014. After a multi-storied career, he more or less retired from journalism in 2015 but still contributes a monthly business piece to the Bradford County Telegraph. He has self-published one non-fiction book and two books of fiction.

RETIRED TEACHERS GLEN TERRY AND FRANCESCA
VIOLICH ENTERTAINED NEIGHBORHOOD CHILDREN WITH
A FRONT YARD "I SPY" GAME, RELYING ON OBJECTS
TAKEN FROM THEIR ATTIC (PHOTO BY GLEN TERRY).

PHILOSOPHICAL AND PSYCHOLOGICAL REACTIONS

ENTERING THE TEMPLE

» BY ERIC DIAMOND

Is gratitude perverse?
for our toxic minute spiked mace intruder,
wafted on the four winds
toward myriad covert entrances,
into a universe of innocent nostrils—

Cryptic disturber of any tranquilities,
relentless mentor, breath teacher,
sage of patience, master of humiliation,
illuminator of shadowy dungeons of terror,
apocalyptic messenger,
pawnbroker of superstition,
postman of desperation and ignorance—

Unveiler of this rude simultaneity,
of angels and monkeys
stunned by waves of plague, surge, and fire,
farmer of compassion's fatigue,
unmasker of the eternal sins,
the callous armor, the coal-cars of hate—

Make us earn every morsel
of equanimitous quiet,
dig our wells of wisdom by hand,
treasure the tingle of contact,
row the Via Negativa of cruel absence—

From Death's visitations
comes the true religion:
humble obeisance to the Great Mother,
supplicating in meaningful suffering
to the Merciful Father,
dissolving clay masks of self-deceit,
dancing naked with Maya,
Radiance and Consciousness

disrobed and emergent,
waltzing and chanting
the Ode to Joy,
then
prostrating on mandala carpets
in the Temple of Life:

Life—
unfathomable, labyrinthine,
immense, exhausting, glorious—
and if good fortune never comes,
here's to whatever comes,
drink *L'chaim*!
to Life!
(dedicated to Rabbi Michael Rose)

THE RICKETY BRIDGE

» BY ADRIAN FOGELIN

I have no expectations beyond this moment. Balanced on the pin-head of now, I make no assumptions about the future, take nothing down the road for granted. This makes the small things that go right feel like gifts—if I don't expect, anticipate, or feel deserving-of, when something good occurs, gratitude washes over me.

The downside is that I don't dare to hope, or let myself look ahead, or plan. The future is a bridge too rickety to imagine walking across, but in truth, has there ever been a bridge at all? The future is never a done-deal until it becomes the past. Maybe that is a truth that has just become more apparent.

Now that I accept this uncertainty, I clutch the moment, do the work of the moment. I call a friend. Wash a dish. Cross a small finite task off a small finite list, a list that would resemble a plan if it were not so immediate and modest…and I keep going…I keep going.

If, now and then, I give up, it is only for a moment. Then the next moment comes along. I discover I am still standing and I take the next step.

I cry more often. Laugh more often. Since the moment is all that is, it hits hard. Sad or happy? Each gets my full attention.

We used to be more connected to each other, more often in each other's company. We had places to go and things to do. It was our collective dreams and efforts that turned the wheels of time. In relative isolation, I lean hard on habits to give the world shape. I walk, stretch, sing scales, and I hold a pen and write my daily pages.

If nothing else, I am a witness, one of many court stenographers recording the unfolding and overwhelming case being argued by the pandemic.

One moment becomes the next, and still I am here. And you are here. And as is always the case, although we are rarely aware of it, this is our moment.

Adrian Fogelin is the author of nine middle-grade and young adult novels all published by Peachtree Publishing in Atlanta. She is also a prolific song writer who performs with her musical partner, Craig Reeder, in a duo called Hot Tamale. Adrian and her husband Ray are riding out the pandemic in their Florida home, Adrian making careful notes on this remarkable time in her many journals.

ON A SHADY LANE

» BY RICHARD GARTEE

On a shady lane, a little boy
picks dandelions, and
leaves them in sweaty bouquets
at the other end of the culvert
for the neighbor girl
who is contagious
and can't come near him
or so their mothers say

His heart wants to tear from
his chest and rush toward her
but they stand
separated by thirty feet of gravel
while the blossoms wither
and their stems curl

*Previously published in the *Ann Arbor Review*

Richard Gartee is an award-winning novelist who has also authored seven college textbooks, six novels, five collections of poetry, and a biography. Two of his novels, *Ragtime Dudes in a Thin Place* and *Ragtime Dudes Meet a Paris Flapper* each won Royal Palm Literary Awards. His poetry regularly appears in *Ann Arbor Review* and elsewhere.

HOPE IS AN INVESTMENT IN THE FUTURE

» **BY ADRIAN FOGELIN**

It takes a chance on disappointment as it leaps toward an imagined joy. But when the future has the potential to be just days long, we can't risk such an investment.

The saying, *make a plan, make God laugh*, feels suddenly prescient. If we have learned anything from the virus, it is that we are not in charge, so why jinx ourselves?

For now, the joy of achieving an outcome based on planning and hard work, even the joy of things remembered, is largely unavailable. I don't imagine myself performing on some future stage, and when a moment from a past performance flashes up, it hurts. Will there ever be a time when my duo, Hot Tamale, can play for a gaggle of folks standing carelessly close to each other, maybe even dancing?

I try not to remember or imagine seeing our daughter, her husband, and our two grandsons. Getting to New Jersey seems suddenly like a voyage off the edge of a flat earth.

But there is a second, more spontaneous form of joy, one not predicated on hope, that is *more* abundant than usual in this time of crisis. It is not the joy that comes of a hope coming to fruition, it is a momentary joy, one that takes us by surprise, a moment of joy we might have been too busy to fully experience, or even notice before the coronavirus.

This joy comes, not from an investment of hope paying off, but from an unexpected source, the joy overtaking us without anticipation or planning because we are moving mindfully enough, slowly enough, to notice the sudden breathtaking beauty of something as small as an ant walking across the vast plain of a leaf on a plant in the yard.

Stilled and slowed, we take the time to really see what is around us. This is a byproduct of the disruption of our normal routines, but it may also be a byproduct of vigilance. We are fully awake and really observing our surroundings, scanning for threats, and in the process we see *all* things with fresh eyes. Who knew the world was so beautiful?

Joy also comes from humor that surprises us, makes us laugh when we are close to tears. Those around us buck us up, not by being profound, but by being ridiculously human.

Our pets are even better at this kind of bucking up. They didn't get the memo about the pandemic, and so they continue to entertain us—and we have the time to pay attention.

When the realization of a hope, which always involves planning and imagining, is impossible, joy *has* to take us by surprise, and it must be complete in itself. It can't remind us of all we have lost, or propose an outcome in an imagined future.

Joy is sized to match what is possible. Right now it comes in the smallest of packages:

a beautiful butterfly flitting past the kitchen window, a bird splashing in the birdbath, a two-year-old grandson saying, "How are you guys doin'?" his face big on the screen.

We hope to hope again sometime in a future we are deliberately not imagining. (Why make God laugh?) Until then, we subsist on moments of joy. Like grace, they come unexpected, unplanned, and unearned.

For once, we are present enough to receive them, and they sustain us.

A DREAM

» **BY MARIE Q ROGERS**

I dreamed I was in a room full of people. Vividly, I recall the colors of their clothing. We sat at tables, holding a meeting. Then, to my horror, I realized none of them were wearing masks. Nor was I! I jumped up from the table and rushed out to my car to get my mask.

You cannot catch the virus from unmasked people in a dream, but this brought home to me how much this pandemic experience has changed our perceptions. Sometimes, watching a movie (Netflix, of course, because the theaters are closed), I wince to see people invading one another's personal space, unmasked. I remind myself that the film was shot Pre-COVID. Is this how we will measure our lives? Pre-COVID and Post-COVID?

I always mask up when I enter a building. Some people do, and some don't. I hear accounts from mask-wearers who encounter hostility from anti-maskers when they meet them in public. So far, I have not had such an experience. Perhaps that's because my forays into the outside world are limited. And perhaps I am "forgiven" because I am of the age group that is considered at risk.

Our country has become divided over the coronavirus. Some deniers have become militant. I suspect this is a coping response, their way of dealing with a reality that is so overwhelmingly unreal they have to deny it. Acceptance would be unbearable. Yet COVID-19 is no respecter of politics. Sickness and death strike both camps. We all live in fear.

Maybe I missed the meaning of my dream. We were sitting at tables, making plans. Will the Post-COVID world bring us together at the table? Perhaps in the dream I was glimpsing the future, when once again we will be able to meet in person, make plans, and go on with our lives.

Then another part of my brain interfered, warning me of danger, sending me scrambling for my mask.

It's not yet time to gather unprotected, but the day will come, masks will safely come off. Then we will face the task of healing grieving hearts, bodies ravaged by disease, and a shattered society. We must hold on to hope. Despair is not an option.

INTERVIEW WITH SHEILA PAYNE

» CO-CHAIR, ALACHUA COUNTY LABOR COALITION (CONDUCTED BY RONNIE LOVLER, MATHESON HISTORY MUSEUM, NOVEMBER 22, 2020)

Ronnie Lovler: Sheila, tell us a little bit about yourself.

Sheila Payne: I'm Sheila Payne. I'm sixty-three. We have lived in Gainesville for twelve years, and I became an organizer at the age of fifteen, after I met Cesar Chavez in the fields of Homestead. I met Paul Ortiz when we started helping to organize with farmworkers decades later.

RL: How has COVID impacted you and the people you serve or hope to serve?

SP: The Labor Coalition has put a lot of effort and energy into tenant organizing and eviction work because that's an impact COVID has had on our community. We've been working on housing for probably four years, mostly with renters' rights. We were going to a lot of housing meetings for about a decade. We realized that no one was going to be building more affordable housing. So we thought about focusing on renters' rights, and getting anti-discrimination language into the city and county codes, inspections, code enforcement, and licensing. The renters' rights ordinance was just passed by the city and we are pivoting to the county.

RL: Can you tell us very quickly what this means for people; perhaps just briefly summarize the renters' rights issue?

SP: Basically, this means people cannot be discriminated against because of source of income. So if someone has a housing voucher, they can move into my neighborhood near UF, instead of all being segregated in one area of the county. Also, there can be no discrimination based on gender preference, citizenship, or if you're a survivor of domestic violence. We had someone call that was told by a (prospective) landlord that he would not rent to her because "he didn't need that kind of trouble." She had been a victim of domestic abuse in the past. Also, veterans were being denied the use of VA (housing) benefits.

So during COVID, we continued with that work and moved into eviction work. We send out letters to about forty people a week whose landlords have filed eviction notices with the courts. We mail them information about their rights and about Three Rivers Legal Services. We also send information about the Cares Act.

We're also knocking on doors, despite COVID. We have a lot of young people working on the eviction issue, and I've been going out. We decided we have to actually knock on doors in the communities with high eviction rates and talk to people and invite them to organize into a tenants' union.

RL: How did COVID make things harder?

SP: It's a drag doing Zoom meetings. Every group that I'm associated with, people do not have as much energy for the work if you're not sharing food together, if you're not hugging each other. The plus side is that we've had a lot of people attending the Zoom meetings where we can also do training with them, which is easier for people than meeting in person. We miss tabling at community events.

Some people on the Labor Coalition board like the idea of continuing Zoom meetings because a lot more people can get on. But then, we have lost a lot of community feeling. We have quite a few people we work with in the community on housing and it's hard for them to get on Zoom because of Internet issues.

We had a great membership meeting last month on the court system in Alachua County. Too many people are in jail who are unable to pay cash bond. It is a program we have written a white paper on and are meeting about with other community members.

RL: How did COVID affect you?

SP: Well, it hasn't affected my work because I work outside. But I haven't seen my son or my sister and her family or Paul's family. So there has been a lot of worry about others in the community. And frustration by trying to organize in a vacuum.

RL: Do you think you've gained anything from your COVID experience that will help you and your organization moving forward?

SP: No, I think we're going to have to rebuild. We've done well with the eviction work. We have a lot of energy there. And we've been able to get a lot of stuff passed, like the contract workers' living wage and renters' rights, within the last month. But I'm not sure we could have gotten to that point if we had COVID that whole time, because we did a lot of in-person meetings. I hate not seeing people in person.

RL: Is there anything that you would like to add?

SP: It's been a hard time for people in our country and our community. I guess because many of us also work in the in-person political arena. So we all were out there fighting really hard as individuals to get city, county, state officials who believe the way we do elected so that we can get stuff passed.

We, of course, were involved in the Black Lives Matter movement protests and projects.

Because the Labor Coalition's been around so many decades, we can provide a lot of backup stuff. We have a paid organizer, part time. Right now we have the infrastructure, for instance, to work on the Bail Fund project. Because we're nonprofit, we can be the fiscal sponsor for the Bail Fund, which helps bail people out of jail, and also for the Free Grocery Store that's feeding 100 families a week,

Fridays, I go to the food bank and buy all the food for half the families. So that's rewarding, and that's been during COVID.

The Bail Fund is crucial. We do not think people should be told to pay $2500 bail, then have to sit in jail because they are low wage, especially during a pandemic. There's a lot of people in jail that shouldn't be there, for minor offenses. That's part of the Court Services because they evaluate who should be in jail. Court Services is part of the whole police state here. It's being used to keep people in jail who don't have a lawyer or the money to bail themselves out.

RL: You asked me about my own circumstances going back on campus at UF and Santa Fe where I teach as an adjunct. You said the Labor Coalition is working on campus safety issues in conjunction with other groups around the unsafe reopening at UF.

SP: We are working against furloughs at UF, and face-to-face instruction. We also have a food system project that we're doing on the UF campus that has workers' rights, farmworkers' rights, and equitable wages for local growers.

RL: You're busy. So we should wrap now. So, is there anything more you think we should cover within the context of COVID?

SP: No. I'm saying everybody needs to do something, though, there's a lot of need. You see it, right? Of course, there's so much need, and COVID just accentuated the extreme poverty in Alachua County, and people are desperate.

RL: Thank you.

SP: Thanks, Ronnie.

CHAPTER 7

HUMOR CAN HELP

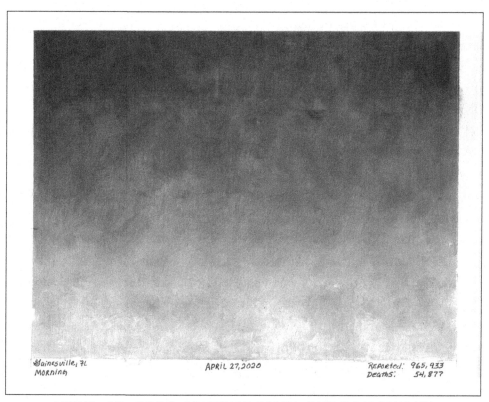

Gainesville, FL
Morning   APRIL 27, 2020   Reported: 965,933
Deaths: 54,877

APRIL 27, 2020 (GWENDOLYN CHRZANOWSKI)

IN THE BEGINNING OF QUARANTINE

» **BY ANN-MARIE MAGNÉ**

My husband and I are hunkered down, obediently staying home and out of harm's way. A wonderful neighbor does our grocery shopping. We leave the house only when absolutely necessary in order to avoid contact with anyone who isn't us.

This sounds like many people's new normal, right? Mundane, boring? We're minding our own business to avoid any problems. But wait, there is no reward for the diligent! Here's what has been going on with us during lockdown, starting with week one in mid-March:

The first thing to poop out on us, pun intended, was the bidet attachment. We got to the bottom of the problem and ordered a new one.

One night both television sets stopped working, simultaneously. No lightning strike, no power outage, just black screens. My husband fiddled with the one in the TV room and managed to get it up and running, but the one in the bedroom … remained fast asleep. A few weeks later the DirecTV tech performed some expensive ritual and got it up and running.

In the meantime, the scheduled maintenance on my car revealed it needed a new tensioner. A what? The replacement caused some tension when we saw the bill.

My husband's computer took a nosedive, so it got a new hard drive. Not to be left behind, my laptop had an aneurysm and needed costly surgery.

The washing machine began making noises unlike anything we'd ever heard. Turns out, they were the sad sounds of mechanical death. No way to fix it, had to buy a new one.

And suddenly the kitchen faucet was wiggly. The base slid from side to side when you turned it on, and water leaked into the cabinet below. More water went down than up. Parts are on backorder, naturally.

Then the salt chlorinator for the pool no longer made saltwater. No swimming allowed. Paying a big repair bill was totally acceptable, though.

I lost a crown on a molar. And swallowed it. No additional information forthcoming. Let's just say I made a good impression and have a new crown.

One of my tires became very good friends with a nut and bolt. Not repairable. Needed a new tire.

At 4 a.m. one morning, my husband threw himself out of bed. He dreamed that he had fallen into a raging river while walking along an icy trail, and was trying to grab the shore to climb out. That escapade earned him seven stitches over his right eye and an awful eight inch gash on his right forearm. Both healed just fine.

The irrigation system became the irritation system, spraying water on the street and driveway. Several sprinkler heads and some other mechanism had to be replaced. By pricey professionals.

Well, the water is perfect but the pool has a leak. Obviously it talked to the kitchen faucet. Estimates on hold for now.

Our security alarm decided we needed to get up at three a.m. a few mornings in a row. A tech came out and replaced some of the contacts. That kept the peace for a week. Another tech visit put the problem on hold briefly. Third time was the charm.

Parts for the faucet arrived—but didn't solve the problem. New faucet on order.

As a reminder that we cannot go out and shop freely like we used to, someone used our credit card for us. The replacement card arrived the day after we were notified, but in the meantime, a few of the automatic payments were declined and my inbox was laced with subtle threats.

My husband's car's passenger side-view mirror fell off. Just fell off. It was caught by the wiring and the handyman who installed the kitchen faucet fixed it. Good thing we needed a new faucet.

I think we're off the calamity carousel. It's been weeks since the last—please be final!—event. Most people would like to resume normal lives, even if it's a slightly different normal. So would we—normal did not include seventeen costly fix-ups in nine weeks. I'm definitely counting our good fortune—wait, the "fortune" now belongs to various other people. Let's just say we're grateful to be healthy, especially after having to interact with so many people as we tried to avoid interacting with people!

However, I have to add, I could've done with a lot more boredom and a lot less excitement. This has not been the quarantine I expected.

Ann~Marie Magné is past vice-president of the Writers Alliance of Gainesville and a current critique-pod leader. In her previous life she worked in sales and customer service, and in 1998 became a Hypnotist. She has published a love story memoir, *Almost Ticked Off*, about her husband's brush with death. She is the mother of one daughter, step-mom to two sons, and Grammy to seven. She loves living in Gainesville, FL with her husband.

(PHOTO BY GREG YOUNG, PRESIDENT, BOARD
OF DIRECTORS, MATHESON MUSEUM)

COVID AND COMMUNITY

» BY MEGAN M. ATWATER

COVID and community. What a funny thing to write and say together. We're all desperately holding on. Holding on to ourselves as parents, as friends, as business owners, and as community members.

If you look at it a certain way, there might not have been a more divisive time. The election is an absolute mess. Even politics in our local community has somehow divided us. (Do you send your kids to school or not? Do you eat out or not?) All in a time when we've never been more isolated.

Yet I'm not writing this article about all of the negative parts of this pandemic. I'm writing it because somehow—in the strangest way—I feel more connected to my community than ever. Maybe it's because I've been forced to really look at what it is that I care about. What it is that makes all of the hard work worth it. I have my specific reasons, and the reasons have to do with my young children. But I think it goes beyond that.

I've always cared about community. About connection. About bringing people together—it brings me significant joy. And somehow in all of this, we've been able to do that more than ever. This article is to point out the beautiful parts. I've never spent more time with my neighbors. My kids play outside and in our local area more than ever. We support local businesses as an intention.

And now we're having a meeting about how to plan a safe but joyful Halloween for our children together. We might end up spacing candy out on a clothesline. And planning a couple of haunted trails with a parent regulating how many children go through. But you know what, we're coming together to make it happen.

In the neighborhood I live in, my neighbor and I have coordinated music and the Sweet Dreams ice cream truck about twice a month since all of this started. And I hope it never stops. Because, while I love going out and seeing friends more than most, being home and knowing my neighbors and connecting with people and us all looking out for each other—that's the stuff we all dream about. About romantic small town living where our children can play and ride bikes and wave at those that live close to them. I love Gainesville, because this is the place I believed could give that to my children. And somehow, in the weirdest way, this pandemic pushed us there.

Megan Atwater is a local realtor and mother of three young children, Everett, Mimi and Mae. She spends most of her time outside and loves the water, but much of her energy is spent on building and maintaining the community of loved ones around her.

HOW A GROUP OF VIRTUAL ANIMALS ON A TROPICAL ISLAND SAVED MY SANITY

» **BY AMANDA ENGEN**

To survive quarantine this summer (2020), like millions of others around the globe, I forged friendships with a bunch of simulated animals on a deserted island, while slowly paying off my mortgage to an overweight tanuki—I played Nintendo's *Animal Crossing: New Horizon.*

Every single day for seven months, this game became a ritual, a bit of normality in a time when things have been anything but normal.

During the summer of 2020, time didn't seem to matter much anymore. Almost in an instant, businesses hung up their closed signs "until further notice." Anxieties and tensions rose both in society and in our cozy 533-square-foot apartment (trust me, we had time to measure). I spent the entirety of lockdown with my husband Michael and our dog Callie. Even when you love someone unconditionally, without the option to pick up and go work at a coffee shop, every keystroke seems to bounce off the paint-chipped walls, breaking our already thin levels of concentration, adding to the frustrations and uncertainty about when things would go back to normal.

Surely, it would be just a couple more weeks.

We like our home, but we like it a lot less when we're told we can't go anywhere else. Other than daily walks to the deserted park with Callie, I only ventured into the real world once a week for a hurried grocery run of whatever meat was left on the shelf and copious amounts of wine. A group chat between friends, typically filled with fun social plans for the week, devolved mostly into reports of hand sanitizer or toilet paper spotted across Gainesville. Life was unrecognizable. Life was dystopian. Life was on lockdown.

Life in *Animal Crossing* was anything but. I had a long list of in-game tasks to do each day. I dutifully picked weeds, caught exotic fish, and excavated fossils all across my small tropical island. The game gave me a reason to get out of bed in the morning. Since the game runs in real time, it quite literally encouraged me to have my life together and moving before the turnip prices changed at noon. My friends and I would run around hunting for rare ironwood furniture recipes, giving us something to chat about other than the terrifying state of affairs engulfing the real world. It served as the ultimate form of escapism in the most peaceful way.

More than that though, the built-in cooperation mechanics of *Animal Crossing* were like a cure for quarantine loneliness. The game allows for friends to visit each other's islands to trade items, or watch meteor showers together, or even exchange NSFW custom designs, so even if we weren't hanging out for the local happy hour, at least we could still make dumb jokes in the game together. My dear college roommate, who now lives in Cincinnati in her own tiny 500-something-square-foot apartment, and I spent many evenings chatting and playing together on the couch, just like we used to, but this time via Zoom. Everything was normal, but not.

Before long, my husband became deeply invested in the complicated genetics of *Animal Crossing* flower breeding. At a time when it seemed like everyone else's backyard quarantine transformations surfaced on our social media feeds, Michael and I found joy and excitement in redesigning our virtual flower beds for a chance to breed rare flowers. It was the closest thing we had to a backyard oasis of our own, and I'm proud to report that at the close of summer that damn elusive blue rose, the rarest flower of all, bloomed on our island.

Quarantine started in chaos, but we eventually found peace with it; so too our island. After 426 hours of play, we've invited all the best villagers to live on our island, excavated every fossil, and paid off our mortgage to the tanuki. From curating a peaceful Zen garden to designing a lavish neon-laden beach bar, to us, our island was complete.

Now, it's been weeks since we've played. And it's not as if the world has gone back to normal. Far from it. But we've settled into this existence. Eight months in and we're entering a new phase of COVID. We're getting used to the "new normal" of socially distant picnics, excitement about the cute new face masks arriving from Etsy, and pets adorably interrupting Zoom meetings. While working from home has brought its own set of complications, I've learned more about work-life balance than I ever thought possible.

This semester, I'm teaching a course at the University of Florida focused on the analytical intersection of gaming and culture. Time and again, my students tell me how they've been able to adjust to the pandemic lifestyle better than most because they have already established these online communities that they're enthusiastic to spend more time in. Whether it's through video chatting with a long-distance friend while peacefully tending to a digital garden, hosting virtual game nights with family, or even raiding a dragon fortress with a bunch of strangers on the Internet, gaming is being used as a tool for interactive socialization throughout the world.

And at a time like this, I'm so thankful to be a part of this community.

Amanda Engen is a Postdoctoral Associate in the University Writing Program at the University of Florida. Most of her teaching and research focuses on the overlap of culture and technology with an emphasis on gaming. Currently, she lives in downtown Gainesville where she walks her dog Callie to Depot Park and plays Pokémon Go every day.

(PHOTO BY CANDY PIGOTT)

"I miss smiles and hugs. Feel sad going to Publix and not being able to smile at others and not seeing others smile back, which explains...my mask."

– Candy Pigott

LEMME OUTTA HERE!

» BY ERIC DIAMOND

I need to move around, I need to expand
Need to see some ocean, need to walk some land
But a nasty little bug is guarding the gate
Saying, "Move your existence to a later date"

I need to hit a party, my mood is turning bitter
I'll gladly stretch some fabric over my viral transmitter
I'll only talk to people from across a fence
I'll carry a sign that says "Keep your F-in' Distance!"

The country boys say pandemic is "just propaganda"
They haven't read Doctor Fauci's memoranda
Some dudes are apparently immune to panic
They'd snicker at the iceberg right in front of the Titanic

Stores are closing, jobs are screwed
If I can't have Lord and Taylor, I'd rather go nude
Evictions are mounting, rents are coming due
Damn this Godzilla version of the old-fashioned flu!

Lose your ticket to the theatre, keep your feet out of the tent
Someone could be hosting a super-spreader event
In the factories and foundries, where they're packing up some meat
In the schoolyard, at the barber, in your office, on your street

I wanna sit at a ballgame, with my hands in my lap
I won't cheer, I won't chortle, I won't root, I won't clap
Just to feel normal, like any other year
I would whimper to the Lord, "Lemme Outta Here!"

Lemme outta here, I'm sick of the plague
I wanna G-O Go! I will beg, beg, beg
I will skulk in the alleys, take a bath in chlorine
I will welcome the needle for a rush-job vaccine

The Kiwis vanquished the virus, there was triumph in Taiwan
The Germans made some progress, with their German aplomb
But when you're all hung up on Rights, over Reason
It makes America great for the killing season!

The price of democracy is eternal vigilance
Checks and balances, earnest diligence
The Founding Fathers would retch and vomit
To see pickpockets pissing on the floor of the Senate

Our common ordeal is dragging on and on
At least it inspired this witty little song
I'm creeping to the market for some sanitized beer
And I'll shout to the heavens, "Lemme Outta Here!"

Lemme outta here, enough of this plague
I wanna G-O Go! I will beg, beg, beg
My internal motor is stuck in low gear
I need some overdrive: Lemme outta here!

GOING WITHIN, LOOKING OUT OR HOW I GOT LOST IN FACEBOOK IN TIMES OF COVID

» **BY J. ELLIOTT**

April:

To be honest, I kick myself that I haven't been more productive. I trust I'm not alone in losing hours a day to sorting through feelings of bewildered distraction, anxiety, and confusion.

I'll confess to spending too much time on Facebook. My dang book has been hanging over me for more than two years. I need to just strap myself to the chair and edit, edit, edit. Yet, instead of easing away from FB as intended, I signed on to more pages. I was intrigued by a page called Kitchen Quarantine—a truly international page where people discussed meal prep in lockdown.

There were two stories that warmed my heart and assuaged the COVID-19 anxiety. The first was from a couple who were just beginning to date when they got confined together in lockdown. Awkward at first, it led to a far deeper exploration of their interests, fears, passions, attitudes. They quickly changed their focus from "well this is awkward" and "how-soon-can-you-go-home?" to "tell me about your family, your childhood, your talents, and-do-you-like artichokes?" and so on. The stuff romance movies are made of. The second story was of a married couple trapped in an apartment in Italy. They already loved each other, but the confinement felt like prison. But soon, the new routine involved spending leisure time snuggling in bed in the mornings, cooking together, singing, playing games. After a few days, they didn't mind the lockdown life. Another love story movie.

More dedicated pages: Classic Ghost Story, Asian Ghosts… I chatted up the admin of that page and *think* I may have sold a book on Amazon Japan! That's a buzz. Another page, The Book of Darkness and Light, product of a clever UK author, Adam Robinson, features polished videos of his stories with sound effects that I aspire to do. He's offering mini writing workshops on FB. I'm excited about this connection.

I've used FB posts as writing prompts. Working on writing more concisely. Yes, it is a delay tactic! I'm sick of editing my book. Comments on FB are like writing warm-up exercises.

What else? Yard work. Housework. Lots of dog walks. Those someday projects like grinding the paint off old lawn chairs and spraying them a cheery Pistachio green.

Editing. I did a word search for "smiled." Eighty-nine of the boogers! He smiled, she smiled, they smiled, oh, *bleck*! Going back to punch them up or delete them. The most recent "she smiled" fix is now "Maggie Beth exclaimed in her gap-toothed, spumante way." (She's a bubbly girl.) I'm down to twenty-nine. Only seventeen grins, thank goodness. That's next. Tomorrow I tackle frowns.

November:

Somewhere after the grim news reports of hospitals around the world filling to capacity subsided, I had a bit of an epiphany. For years I've contemplated doing a Vipasanna retreat in Georgia. This is an intensive, nine-day silent meditation—just an intro to Vipasanna. Believe it or not, some meditations go twenty-one days or longer. Nine days. Sitting in silence. Just you and your thoughts in a room with other people on cushions with their thoughts. I've wanted to do this for years and yet have found excuses—can't take off that much time, animals, unreliable vehicle, blah blah. To be honest, I'm scared. Many people end not being able to complete the nine days. Some tap into very dark places in their psyches and cry a lot. What would I experience? Would I fidget myself right out of the session and bolt for the car? Would I fail?

I live in the country. Stuck at home? Hmm. Epiphany: why not think of it as a modified retreat of choice rather than an imposed lockdown? This lockdown has coffee and chocolate and no pressure to sit still all day! I have no idea how people stuck in tenement housing cope in cities where people are not allowed out except to get groceries. They didn't sign on for Vipasanna.

I have six and a half acres of land to maintain and trails to walk. I'm enjoying it now, but it was none too pleasant over the summer with the heat and mosquitoes. Walking my Basset hounds a few times a day was the extent of my outdoor time. My cat continues to spend more time on the mediation cushion than I do. I did get back to writing in a journal.

Published *Monkey Heart* in September! My #1 fan in Maryland loved it. Worth all of it for that.

The ghost story writing class was a wonderful distraction. A homework assignment inspired a creepy little piece about an orphan haunted by her mother's false teeth. Not long after, a call for submissions for a fable crossed my radar. I polished the story and submitted it. It was accepted! Painted a haunted castle during class. Must write story.

I bought a microphone and video software and learned the basics of making videos. I recorded two of my favorite short stories and made videos of them. Little did I know when I started this project on a whim, bumping and feeling my way towards the kind of videos that Adam Robinson is producing with The Book of Darkness and Light, that it would be useful in making my own video for the Sunshine State Book Festival in January. A fifteen-minute video is required in order to participate. Serendipity! I submitted my video and got feedback that it was "entertaining." All that I could hope for!

I continue to find FB a honey-laced razor. I scroll through the muck, embrace the honey, inspired by the resilience and creativity seeded by adversity.

Through this period, I've gone within physically, focusing on house projects—we got a new roof and a woodstove hooked up; I've rearranged the living room and chucked an old sofa. Mental deep dive—more journal writing, more contemplation, more gratitude.

Much as I hate it sometimes (Sometimes? No, daily!), Facebook has also been a lifeline for contact and creativity.

J. Elliott is a practicing Buddhist, artist, and author living in North Central Florida. She has written three collections of short ghost stories and is working on a funny mystery series beginning with *Monkey Mind*. You can find her on social media under Hedonistic Hound Press.

LIVING IN A DYSTOPIAN NOVEL

» BY MARIE Q ROGERS

They first called it a "novel" coronavirus, but it mutated into a real-time dystopian novel.

2020 arrived innocently enough. While we celebrated the New Year, COVID lurked in the sidelines, waiting to take center stage. Initially only a vague specter, it materialized from the shadows to become a source of ghoulish entertainment, dominating the airwaves. Could this be a replay of 1918? Surely not in this age of medical miracles!

The pundits could not hide their dread. Their knitted brows were enough to freeze my spine. Older ladies of my acquaintance quarantined themselves. It was rumored this would become everyone's fate. But surely that couldn't happen, could it? Then came March.

On Friday the 13th, the world changed. Schools closed. People stopped going to work. Panicked hordes stripped grocery shelves clean—of toilet paper, no less! Meetings, travel plans, weddings, and funerals were cancelled. Life, once plotted out in calendar entries, became a fogged-up windshield in a vehicle out of control, hurtling at unknown speed to a nebulous future. That's when I realized I was living inside a dystopian novel.

Stories and movies came to mind, of catastrophic events that spell the end of the world: wars, alien invasions, plagues decimating the world's population. In some stories, heroes emerge to save remnants of humankind. In others, the heroes are lucky to save themselves. Great entertainment for us, dystopian stories are no fun for the besieged characters. And now I was a character in one.

As a writer, it's not such a bad place to be as long as my retirement checks keep coming, the electric grid holds up, and I can get groceries every week or so. If the electricity fails and I can't go shopping, I'd survive on my cache of hurricane supplies. But, darn, if I couldn't use my computer, I'd have to resort to old fashioned pen and paper.

I discovered how much I depend on technology. One day, my phone stopped working. Good, no spam calls. I still had internet. A week later, phone service restored, the internet went out! I nearly panicked—a character in a movie, surrounded by unknown perils, communication with the outside world cut off!

The first week of quarantine was disconcerting. The second, I settled into the unreality of it and watched the movie play out around me. But the surreal turned bizarre when the world began to morph into *my* dystopian novel.

My soon-to-be-published dystopian novel, *The Season of the Dove*, takes place in the future when solar power has replaced fossil fuels, but it didn't happen soon enough. South Florida has gone the way of Atlantis and autocrats build houses that can withstand

Category 7 hurricanes. Books aren't banned, but they're obsolete. Information is stored digitally, making it easy to rewrite history.

In my book, the US has been partitioned into autonomous regions, each with its own set of laws. When a killer hurricane strikes, Georgia closes its border to keep Florida refugees out. Hospitals run out of supplies and the sick and injured crowd hallways and cover the floors. The poor are hardest hit and the rich see the devastation as an opportunity to enrich themselves.

Until the pitchforks come out…

My novel is a fantasy, a series of events that won't come to pass. Will they?

Coastal communities already deal with sea level rise. Hurricanes are becoming more powerful. The advent of hurricane season in this plague year sent my fellow Floridians' anxiety levels off the chart.

As COVID-19 went viral in New York, hordes of Yankees headed south to escape. Rumors circulated that Florida was setting up roadblocks to keep them, and their contagion, out. When the tide turned and Florida became a hot spot, the northern states rolled up their welcome mats. Hospitals were over capacity and undersupplied. An economic bailout ensured that rich corporations made out like bandits while the rest of us were thrown crumbs.

I'd finished my first draft long before all this, and I never expected to see it happen. Each development has given me pause. Just coincidence? I'm certainly no prophet.

A public official gave out erroneous information and his government website was altered to align with what he'd said. Rewriting history is not a new idea. Remember *1984*?

In my novel, when the peasants revolt, those in power call out the National Guard. A few soldiers express disgust—they were trained to fight foreign enemies, not their own countrymen.

In our world, after George Floyd's murder, we peasants protested. When dissent was accompanied by violence, the troops were called out. Yikes! A few military officers disagreed with using them to control civilians.

In my book, Texas was the first to secede from the US. After the recent election, they are actually threatening to do so. Self-styled "law abiding" states are also talking about forming their own confederations in opposition to states they see as having different values and goals.

My heroes encounter "post offices," remnants of the USPS, which had been replaced by private companies that don't serve rural communities, isolating them. In our world, the Postmaster General, who owns stock in private companies, tried to defund our Postal Service.

Not all is gloom and doom. My heroes encounter good people, many of them have-nots, who share what they have. Even some of the well-to-do show their charitable sides.

In the current pandemic, people have stepped up to contribute what they can to those in need. Mom and Pop restaurants feed the hungry. Ladies with sewing machines stitch up face masks. The food bank business is booming, with contributions as well as assistance. It's refreshing to see that compassion and service survive in in our present dystopia, as well as in fictional ones.

I'll tell you, though, if more elements of my book come to pass in real life, I will have to rewrite it. Maybe as a cozy romance? Or a history? What could be the harm in that?

*Previously published in marieqrogers.com

CHAPTER 8

COVID AND CREATIVITY

April 29, 2020 (Gwendolyn Chrzanowski)

MASQUE TWO: A PUPPET SHOW

» BY CHARLOTTE M. PORTER

Chorus Line: The Frogs
Cast of Characters: All wear masks and social distance

Old Normal, Aristophanes, elder bullfrog, masked, on his pad with a cane.

Hermit, millennial bullfrog, masked, on his pad.

Bella, frog with pretty markings and bangles, masked, on her pad with her makeup kit.

Same Old Crowd (SOC), frog chorus, green head to toe, with spats and face shields.

Scene: A pond of giant lily pads with recorded nature sounds. Facing the audience, **Aristophanes** and **Hermit** squat on their respective pads (round felted skateboards) and harbor votive lights. They swat bugs, pull out their long tongues like bubble gum, and stretch their legs with webbed feet (scuba frog fins). **Bella** reclines on her pad on her elbow as if a diva on a daybed. Behind them, **Same Old Crowd** defines the pond and functions as chorus. They are frogmen.

FADE in

Same Old Crowd line-dance in rhythm with a recorded frog chorus of COVID, COVID.

Hermit: Hey, Aristophanes, what with Climate Change, how's your pad treating you?

Aristophanes: Past bloom, Hermit, but thanks for asking. And you?

Hermit: Like normal, I'm beating skeeters, ha, ha, to beat the heat.

Same Old Crowd line-dance in recorded frog chorus.

Hermit: Listen to them boys. They sure can swingle.

Bella: Stag dance in social isolation, more like it. Poor fellas, they're looking for a kiss.

Aristophanes: (cocks his head, raises his cane) Rain soon.

Bella: Change your tune. I don't want to hide my light under a bushel.

Hermit: What's up your way, Bella?

Bella: Real estate, flipping houses, but the market's real slow in a plague year.

Same Old Crowd line-dance to recorded frog chorus, COVID, COVID.

Bella: Rowdy, eh, pent-up. This year, no high-school prom night, no moonlight stroll.

Aristophanes: Noisy, whipper-snappers. I need ear pads to hear myself think.

Hermit: Move over. Social distance. Just a tad, ha, ha.

Same Old Crowd chorus, COVID, COVID.

Aristophanes: So, Bella, dear, where are the Tadpoles?

Bella: The Poles, the little darlings? (lifting her pad edge) Down under, testing their gills.

Hermit: Like they're fish. Well, tads will be tads...

Aristophanes: Will be frogs, the next generation. Speaking of poles, we all need to vote, mail-in or swim-in. Do it!

Hermit: Support clean water initiatives. Our youngsters need a safe clean world.

Bella: For now, underwater breath, a mother's gift, gets them off-pad, out of the house.

Hermit: These days, so much trash and run-off, I'm chicken to stay under too long.

Same Old Crowd chorus, COVID, COVID.

Bella: That's why these fab legs (showing off her gams) and world-famous kick.

Aristophanes: (recites) *Alas, fleet-footed time leaves webbed age on edge.*

Bella: I used to have trim thighs and a waistline. Now I'm embarrassed to wear shorts in public.

Aristophanes: In that regard, masks help.

Bella: What can I say?

Aristophanes: To rephrase an ancient poet, *Not for me the honey or the sting.*

Hermit: Not to mention the night Giggers...

Aristophanes: (interrupts) Hermit, how I wish you wouldn't use the G-word for armed humans.

Good friend, you know better. Don't hide behind your mask to tongue-wag.

Bella: (painting her toes) Say what you want, Aristophanes, but armed killers in airboats roam the lake, our lake, our community...

Hermit: Looking to flour our legs for French stew.

Aristophanes: In World War II, the Greatest Generation called the French Frogs.

Hermit: Without *voulez-vous*, if you please, melted butter, ha, ha.

Same Old Crowd chorus, COVID, COVID.

Bella: (looking up from her pedicure) How did GI flat-foots appropriate *our* bragging rights?

Aristophanes: My dear Bella. Exercise *your* First Amendment Rights. Are you registered to vote?

Hermit: This year, we're doing a call-in, ha, ha.

Same Old Crowd chorus, COVID, COVID.

Bella: An all-night lily pond shout-out, to make our voices count...

Hermit: And spare us from the Grim Gig..err Gourmet Chef, ha, ha.

Same Old Crowd chorus, COVID, COVID.

Aristophanes: Chorus is swan song, the *sous saucier,* alas, the syrup before Death, the final croak.

Hermit: The honey and the sting.

Bella: So, Aristophanes, good elder, lose the bad mood, get upbeat (dipping her webbed toes). He who laughs last, laughs best.

Hermit: (buzzing) Bee fun.

Aristophanes: I am too old. I wear my trousers rolled (rolls up his pad edges), but I'm ready for change. I'm not scared to get my feet wet. (Aristophanes waves his cane and suddenly dives over the edge with a big splash.)

Bella: (hands up in alarm) Golly, goodness, Aristophanes is off to chorus. Who knew the old geezer still had that sweet stuff in him? (bats her eyes in disbelief, shakes her head, opens her lily umbrella)

Hermit: (scratches his head in amazement) Old Froggy's off a-courtin'. And no belly flop, no sir-ree. Seeking the sweet spot, he is, and best of luck at the Villages. In the plague year, romance is what it is, ha, ha (opens his mouth, hangs a grand tongue, holds out his hands).

Rain drops fall. **Same Old Crowd** hoofs and turns *Singing n the Rain* to an upbeat COVID, COVID, chorus in line-dance, joined by the cast for final bow with wet **Aristophanes** holding gloved hands with a beautiful goldfish. They give each other and the audience big air-kiss smooch.

FADE out

THE END

Award-winning fiction author, Charlotte M. Porter, lives and writes in an old Florida citrus hamlet. This masque was one of a series of short plays critiqued in a Writers Alliance of Gainesville (WAG) pod. In the time of COVID, readers, seeking some light-hearted relief, can enjoy the pun of pod and lily pad. The author wishes to thank other WAG members for their valuable critiques. She especially acknowledges the thoughtful comments of the late Daniel South.

"Beginning in late March [2020], I have put out an art project in my driveway every other week. So far, there have been four, and I am putting out the next one this week."

– Peggy Halsey, retired Global Program Director
for the United Methodist Denomination.

BEGINNER'S MIND

» BY MARY BAST

Over my lifetime a variety of teachers have helped me better understand myself, especially with models for creativity and creative thinking. My own creativity leans toward making the present better, but I greatly admire and sometimes enter that space where a new possibility emerges. This innovative space, which decries any rules, defies prediction, and shows up only if I'm in beginner's mind, opened to me during the early pandemic days of isolation. I was simply doodling with colored pens on a sketch pad while sitting on the patio with my cats, smelling the air, feeling peaceful, in a meditative state, being present.

Not once did I start out thinking I'd draw a particular shape. Only when a sketch felt complete did I stop, mentally step back, and "see" something. These drawings, which I came to refer to as my "pandemic totems," not only helped relieve my anxieties about COVID-19, they also led me to reminisce about the many joys of my so-far-long life. Then, having achieved their purpose, they left.

I loved their visits and look forward to another surge of unplanned creativity, which I know from experience will take an entirely unexpected form. The snake, for example, is not quite like any of the other drawings, so there was no precedent for its winding shape. True to its form, Snake Totem helps us look in all directions, listening, watching the environment carefully to know when to act.

Doodem

While exploring possible meanings for the figures that were showing up in my drawings, I learned that the Ojibwe word for *totem* is *doodem*—the perfect word for my *doodles*. Bear Totem was my very first *doodem*.

Bear represents the strength and courage that come from grounding ourselves in the face of adversity. That grounding helps us find our path and journey.

Sniff Out Problems, Seek Answers

I've never had a dog as a pet. In my only childhood memory of a family dog, when I was four or five years old, I'd been given the task of walking a cow to the river to drink (my dad taught high school agriculture before he joined the Army when I was six). On my way back from the river, holding the rope that was tied to the cow's neck, our dog stood up in front me and put its paws on my shoulders. I didn't like it, but don't remember being scared, and I've never been afraid of dogs, just not interested in having one for a pet.

So, I was surprised when I kept coming back to one of my sketches during the early months of isolation, each time thinking, "It's a dog … no, I'm not sure … " until I could no longer ignore it. This totem symbolizes to me a happy dog, kind of chubby, tail wagging, standing on hind legs with front paws about to reach out, maybe from that distant memory of the family dog putting its paws on my shoulders.

Dog Totem reminds us to sniff out problems, seek answers.

Celebrate!!!

I've viewed many videos of cockatoos dancing and my favorite continues to be Snowball (viewable on YouTube). Though my Cockatoo Totem isn't white like Snowball, when I saw its crest and dancing feet, I immediately knew it was a cockatoo.

Most of my life others might have seen me as a "serious" person. I have a poker face and don't smile easily, even though firecrackers and bright lights might be exploding from sheer joy within me. If you saw my paintings, though, you'd find what my friends call a certain "Mary-ness," a slightly offbeat, humorous quality.

Thus, I was delighted to be reminded by the Cockatoo Totem how important it is to celebrate spontaneity, to feel joy and bring light into all our relationships—especially important when we can't be together in person.

Await a New Beginning

Here in Gainesville, Florida, we have plenty of gators, including the University of Florida's football team. Curious how the team got its name, I found that Phillip and Austin Miller introduced UF pennants with alligator emblems at their Gainesville store in 1908, without any input from the university. Students started buying the pennants and three years later, in 1911, the Florida football team began calling itself the "Gators."

So, of course an alligator was destined to appear among my totems to heal pandemic fears. Alligator Totem heals by embracing and working through emotions so we can patiently await a new beginning.

Believe in Miracles

I've been stung twice by a bee, and I remember both vividly. The first time, I was a fifth grader visiting a Shinto shrine with my family, in Tokyo, Japan, where my father was stationed after World War II. It was during warm weather, I was wearing a cotton blouse, and a bee flew up one of my sleeves and stung hard. The second time I was in my twenties, playing nine holes of golf in Cincinnati, Ohio. Because I hadn't played in a long time my golf shoes wore a blister on one foot, so I took off my shoes and planned to finish the round barefoot. Almost immediately, I stepped on a bee and it stung the bottom of my foot! Yikes!!!

Already loving bees for their honey, in more recent years I've also come to understand and appreciate their crucial role in the ecosystem, which far outweighs any negative memories of bee stings. And when this totem appeared among my isolation doodlings, I read more about bees, discovering that—structurally—they shouldn't be able to fly.

Of course, bees fly anyway, and thus Bee Totem reminds us to believe in miracles.

Mary Bast, Senior Editor of *Bacopa Literary Review*, has published poetry, found poetry, and memoir in a variety of print and online journals. Her works include *Autobiography Passed Through the Sieve of Maya* and the poetry chapbooks *Eeek Love, Time Warp, Unmuzzled, Unfettered, and Toward the River*. Recently retired from her career as a leadership consultant and Enneagram coach/mentor, Bast has authored or co-authored five professional Enneagram books. She is also an artist and Membership Chair of the Gainesville Fine Arts Association.

TENDERNESS

» **BY LOLA HASKINS**

When the pandemic began and I was told I could leave the house only on essential errands, I thought I'd be fine. Like most writers, I'm an introvert. And besides, ever since 2004 when my marriage ended, I've lived alone, so I'm used to it. And besides that, I have both relatives and dear long-term friends who love me, and I love them.

At first I *was* fine, because sheltering in place started me on such a roll, that over the first three months, I came up with a series like nothing else I've written. Its subjects are seeds, wind, the sea, prairie, and fire. Poems about our arrogance as a species followed that. And then, after a few comic "panku," tiny observations different from others I've made, because these came to me only when my walks became meditations.

But as the roll subsided, I began to miss the physical presences of the people I love, most of all my son, daughter, and grandchildren. Django's Arden, age two, started to talk, and his Silas, six, began to read, and I wasn't there to praise them. D'Arcy's Lyddy, fifteen, made story boards for the film she'd planned to shoot this summer but I haven't seen those either, nor her, nor her sister Ava who's eighteen and for months has seen her boyfriend only from separate cars. And we three—she and Zack and I—had been having so much fun—spaghetti for dinner, followed by games with lots of trash-talking across the table. I miss that, too. But what I think has been the hardest thing for me of all the hard things has been being denied hugs, kisses and—though those haven't been with me for a while—the possibility of someone stroking my cheek or rubbing my back, or, in the middle of the night, touching my foot with his.

After feeling sorry for myself, aka wallowing for a while (at that point I was selfish enough to ignore the fact that there were thousands if not millions of people in my exact situation and that all of us were deeply lucky), I started looking for something to make me feel less sad. For many, the solution would have been a pet. But since in real life I travel, it wasn't mine. I tried Zooming, but watching people I love on TV left me even more lonely. What finally mended my heart was holding trees. I have four regulars. I put my arms around each of them, lean in, and when I can clearly feel their spirits against my body, sap against heartbeat, I pat their trunks with both hands, kiss them lightly, pat them again, and say, "See you soon." Here's a poem. Read it, then I'll tell you what happened next.

100,000 Lives
When I hold you my hands do not meet
behind.

When I press my cheek against your bark
I am asking you

to mark me. When I lean into you
you rise towards

the light. Grandfather, thank you
for your calm.

I have been so afraid.

Though the poem felt deeply private when I wrote it, I thought later that it might help someone else who, like me, had never thought of trees as consolations. It had been accepted by *Gargoyle,* a magazine in Washington DC, in December 2020, but since the issue wouldn't come out until May, 2021, it wouldn't have been seen when it was most needed. Besides, I thought it needed to reach more people, especially people who don't usually read poems. Then I had an *Aha* moment: what about the *New York Times*?

I'd never have pursued it if a friend hadn't told me ages ago that the current poetry editor, Naomi Shihab Nye, liked my work. And because I love what *she* writes—deep, genuine, and beautiful—I checked it out and found a couple of interviews in which she'd mentioned me by name. So what the hell, I thought. This isn't about me anyway, so what do

I have to lose? Because her e-mail's not public, I wrote her booking agency, saying, "Don't pass this note along if you don't want to." But they did want to, and she wrote me right back. We've since become friends, and she's at least as nice as I'd always heard she was. But, she said, though she loved the poem, she couldn't use it because the *NYT* confines her to spotlighting poetry from new books. She asked me if I had one of those, to which I said, not exactly. There's *Asylum* (my Pitt book), but it was published last year. On the other hand, it *had,* like lots of people's books I imagine, been zapped by the pandemic, so might she consider that.

Well, after she checked with the *Times,* she said yes, she could. So she featured "Hedgehog" *and* my book in her column. And since the *NYT* has the highest circulation of anything I've ever had to do with, whether being in the Sunday magazine resulted in sales or not (as it turned out, it didn't, but it's still okay), it rescued my depression over a book I was sure had failed. And none of that would have happened, because without COVID and that poem ("100,000 Lives"), I'd have way been too shy to approach Naomi.

A couple weeks after the *NY Times,* a plumber came to fix my sink. When he asked me how I was doing, I told him I'd found something that helped, but he'd think I was crazy. He said in no uncertain terms that he wouldn't, so I got brave and told him the poem. He then asked for a signed copy which he took home, saying he'd put it on his Instagram account. A couple of weeks later, I was out walking and an SUV stopped beside me and JB shouted out the window, "YOUR POEM IS AWESOME!" and "AND MY GIRLFRIEND HERE LOVES IT TOO!!" And when he had to come back, just this week, to fix my toilet, he told me he still carries the poem around with him in his truck. What more could any poet ask?

After JB, came Ray, an older man up the street, who wanted a copy for his church, and my sweet Italian student, who asked if I'd mind if she shared it with her friends back in Italy. All of which goes to show that poetry really *is* for everyone. Furthermore, it joys me that this particular poem has had the chance to bring the power and beauty of trees to a few people who might otherwise have passed them without noticing. As for my part, I still visit Grandfather and his kin because I know that they will always be as salvational and glorious to me as they are now.

Lola Haskins lives in Gainesville, Florida. Her poetry has appeared widely, both in the US and abroad, and has been broadcast on both NPR and BBC. She has published fourteen collections of poems, a poetry advice book, a book of fables about women (illustrated by Maggie Taylor) and a non-fiction book about fifteen Florida cemeteries (University Press of Florida). She retired from teaching Computer Science at the University of Florida in 2005 and served from then until 2015 on the faculty of Rainier Writers Workshop.

AFTER ANOTHER VIRTUAL MEETING

» BY J. BRENT CROSSON

I go out back
And lie in the grass
Everything's gone online
But the spring's been held back

Each bud above me
Held static on a naked branch

But connected by the network of branches
We go on wirelessly talking
And freezing up and
Thawing out on warm days
Like this in the grass

Can you hear me?
I'm sitting up now
So as to show you how
The evidence of red bleeds through
The backlit network of branches
As black as old fishing nets
That hang like destiny
Manifest as the end

That's the furnace in the west
Where the test-sites and forests
Still burn at a social distance
And now the country can't unquarantine

These are the lies that wire us together
There is a furnace
But there's no red menace
Only bands of orange clouds
That trail off like surf
Surrendering to the west

Only a network of branches without nets
Above a screen
Of dormant vines
Covering a fence
That defines
What we rent
From those that stole it

My landlord calls me
From the other side of the fence
Swearing he's not contagious
But confessing to loneliness
Through the lattice
Of chain link and vines

This is our experience of exile
However small

We talk through the screen that separates us
The privacy agreement that only the branches above us transgress
But they are caught in leafless expressions
Frozen as if trying to re-connect

J. Brent Crosson is Associate Professor of Religious Studies at UT Austin and a native of Gainesville, FL where he grew up. His book *Experiments with Power* is published by University of Chicago Press, and his poetry has appeared in *Anthropology and Humanism, American Religion,* and *Bacopa.*

PANDEMIC BLUES

» BY ERIC DIAMOND

This pandemic is a pain in my ass
This pandemic is a pain in my ass
I cannot get no sleep
With the virus on a creep
This pandemic is a pain in my ass

They tell me that society's been cancelled
They tell me that society's been cancelled
I'm hangin' in my room
Because society's on Zoom
This pandemic is a pain in my ass

Can't remember what a hug even feels like
Can't remember what a hug even feels like
Got an itching on my skin
And my patience's wearing thin
This pandemic is a pain in my ass

New York is in a natural-born disaster
New York is in a natural-born disaster
There's a wicked case of flu
Out on Seventh Avenue
This pandemic is a pain in my ass

The Black Plague was a shit-show there in Europe
The Black Plague was a shit-show there in Europe
Nineteen-eighteen was killer
Twenty-twenty's killer-diller
This pandemic is a pain in my ass

Mr. Virus won't you mutate down to nothin'?
Mr. Virus won't you mutate down to nothin'?
We got whiskey in a flask
But we're running out of masks
This pandemic is a pain in my ass

Every country's got a lion's share of trouble
Every country's got a lion's share of trouble
There's dyin' all around
For the white, the black, the brown
This pandemic is a pain in my ass

This pandemic is a pain in my ass
This pandemic is a pain in my ass
I cannot get no sleep
With the virus on a creep
This pandemic is a pain in my ass

Chords

E

E7   B7

E7

A7

E7 B7 E

LIVING THE ARTIST'S LIFE

» BY MALLORY M. O'CONNOR

Since we first met in Spring, 1962, my husband John and I have shared a passion for art. But we have also cherished another enthusiasm that has played a significant role in our lives together: great food. We both love to cook (and to EAT), so a couple of years ago we decided to collaborate on a project that combines two of our favorite topics: a memoir/cookbook focusing on our dual careers as artists and food-lovers. I would write the text and John would illustrate the various recipes with his own original works of art. There was only one problem, when were we going to have the time to take on this truly monumental endeavor?

Enter COVID-19. Self-quarantining at home over the past year has given us the perfect opportunity to work almost non-stop on this beautiful "trip down memory lane." We have had uninterrupted time to research the journals that I have kept since 1962, documenting our favorite celebrations, to locate old photos and information on our family and friends, and to copy down recipes from a variety of sources, including my mother's files and John's recollections of celebrations from his childhood. It also provided time for John to set to work creating a series of pastel paintings of the various recipes we wanted to include in the book.

Back in 1963, not long after John and I were married, he took me to meet two artist friends of his who would have a significant influence on me. William Theo Brown and his partner, Paul Wonner, lived in a lovely house in Malibu overlooking the Pacific Ocean. I was enchanted by their beautiful home and the serene surroundings. We had lunch on a terrace overlooking the ocean and dined on the simple but perfectly prepared food that Paul provided: a delicious cheese omelet, fresh greens from the garden, and for dessert, a luscious strawberry Bavarian cream.

On our next visit, I asked Bill what career path he thought I should follow, and he replied, "Live the artist's life." For years I pondered over his advice. What did it mean to "live the artist's life?" I finally came to realize that there were no written codes, no hard and fast rules. You didn't have to starve in a garret or drink yourself to death or cut off your ear. You didn't even have to literally "make art" *physically*. The *art* was your *life*—your values, your outlook, your point of view. It was the things you cherished, whether they were people or places or ideas.

Easter Sunday, 2020, is definitely one we'll always remember. For one thing, it was the thirty-sixth day of "sheltering in place" from the COVID-19 virus. We had planned to spend Easter week with our son and daughter-in-law in Chattanooga, but the pandemic prompted a change of plans. As it turned out, that was not such a bad thing after all, since Chattanooga was hit Easter night by an EF-3 tornado with estimated wind speeds up to 145 mph. It was on the ground for fourteen minutes and traveled fourteen and a half miles from southeast Chattanooga to Ooltewah. The tornado killed three and injured nineteen. It was only one of the 105 tornados that struck the Southeast over the Easter weekend. Fortunately, Chris and Eli were not injured. They suffered only minor damage to their home, although they lost power for three days. Several of their friends were not so lucky.

In lieu of our planned trip to Tennessee, John and I decided to have our own Easter Brunch to celebrate the Spring of our Discontents. We were together. We were safe. And we had lots more to be thankful for. So, even though the past year has been a strange and disturbing time in our collective history, for us it has been time well spent remembering all the good times we've had with friends and family—cooking, eating, making art, and living the artist's life.

(© JOHN A. O'CONNOR, COEUR A LA
CRÈME, PASTEL ON PAPER, 2020)

John A. O'Connor, 81, taught art at the University of California-Santa Barbara; Ohio University, Athens; and the University of Florida, Gainesville, until his retirement in 2005. His service included a number of administrative positions including Director of the Appalachian Center for Crafts and Director of the UF Center for the Arts and Public Policy. He has had thirty-six solo exhibitions of his paintings and his art is in many public and private collections.

EDITOR BIOGRAPHY

Pat Caren is a retired teacher and social worker who studied Literature at Eckerd College and did graduate work at the University of Florida. She has been a member of the Writers Alliance of Gainesville since 2013 including a term as President from 2019 to 2020.

Charles Cobb serves on the Board of the Matheson Museum. He is a curator and archaeologist at the Florida Museum of Natural History.

Ronnie Lovler is a freelance writer and editor and a contributing writer for the Gainesville Sun. She serves as an adjunct professor at the University of Florida and Santa Fe College. She is a former correspondent for CNN in Latin America was also a Knight International Journalism Fellow in Colombia

Mallory M. O'Connor, holds degrees in art, art history, and American history from Ohio University. She taught art history at the University of Florida and Santa Fe College for over twenty years. She is the author of two non-fiction books and six novels.

Print
by Ba

d in the United States
ker & Taylor Publisher Services